CW00505414

The Exodus Pharaoh

How and why one of the greatest
stories of the bible really happened

by

Colin Jaque

Shield Crest

ISBN: 978-1-915657-26-8

MMXXIII

A CIP catalogue record for this book
is available from the British Library

Cover picture shows The Goddess Ma'at

Published by
ShieldCrest Publishing Ltd.,
Aylesbury, Buckinghamshire,
HP22 5RR   England
Tel: +44 (0) 333 8000 890
www.shieldcrest.co.uk

I owe a debt of gratitude to Lord Jonathan Sacks who prompted me to carry out the investigation that has led to this book. Having told him that I could not understand how anyone could have concluded that Ramesses II was Pharaoh of the Exodus, he pointed my attention to the fact that one had to take a positive attitude and explain who that King was and why. This attracted my interest, and with my legal training I hope that I have achieved that aim, and at least provided a new and realistic approach to a subject that has tested the abilities of so many experts over some 2,500 years.

I would also wish to acknowledge the forbearance of my wife, Avril, and members of my family and friends who have had to live through the efforts I had to make while researching this book.

INTRODUCTION

As children we are all introduced to the Bible stories, and we pass on those tales to our own children and grandchildren. They are the most popular stories ever written which is not surprising because they contain all the drama, excitement and pathos that we could desire. But in recent years many have taken a more active part, some trying to prove the veracity of the events, and others endeavouring to show that they are simply myths.

For my own part I found the result of investigations by both experts and amateurs alike most interesting. Many of their arguments which differ in so many ways have force, and some seven years ago I began to carry out my own research which led me to believe that the vast majority of the conclusions reached were simply disproved by the known facts.

The Exodus excited my curiosity because I felt sure that it was true, but the story left important facts omitted with so much untold. There is no indication given of the date when this important event occurred, and the Bible is even silent on the name of the Pharaoh who was involved. The consensus of opinion for the last 2,500 years by the involved experts, historians and academics is that it was Ramesses II who confronted Moses, but this seemed to me to be without any realism if only because of that King's great age. It was hardly likely that, at the grand old age of 92, he would have jumped on the back of a chariot to chase escaping slaves across the desert. The problem was how to prove that the events actually occurred when so many had tried and failed.

There was no point in producing an answer that known facts and the latest discoveries could disprove, and it would be pointless to maintain a theory which could only be proved by making changes to the scant evidence that does exist. Equally so, the story in the Bible had to take account of the social, political and economic events in Egypt at the time. It must be remembered that the Bible stories had until the time of Moses simply been passed down from father to son by word of mouth and were only intended to be a record that was relevant to the Habiru tribe (as the Israelites were then known) to make the history attractive to the children of the tribe and to give them pride in their heritage. It is also relevant to point out that Egypt at the time had a habit of only recording events that showed the regime in the best possible light and the Exodus was a disastrous embarrassment for them.

I decided that the only way was to take what evidence there is in the Bible and to see how that could be fitted into the known history of ancient Egypt. My study of this part of Egyptian history holds a fascination for me, as the people had formulated a Code of Conduct which I soon realised was to form the whole basis of modern religion as we now know it and which Freemasonry seeks to emulate. Putting the history of Egypt and the Habiru tribe together has produced the most fascinating story and gives an explanation to the whole series of events so vividly bringing them to life.

To achieve this result it was necessary to ascertain the full details of the events that took place tracing the history of the Habiru tribe from Abram (later called Abraham) through to Joseph, and to consider the terrible problems facing the Egyptians at the end of the 17th Dynasty and to appreciate the reason for the initial contact between them and the advantage to both of joining forces to defeat the joined forces of the Hyksos (a tribe that had emanated from Asia and settled in the Delta region of Egypt) and the Kushites (a tribe from Nubia, south of the Egyptian border), which would otherwise have undoubtedly led to the annihilation of both Egypt and the Habiru.

It is also important to understand why, 150 years later, the Egyptians were to turn on the Israelites, reducing their status in society, eventually enslaving them.

Within the confines of this book lies a tale of human endeavour to build a nation and a way of life perfect in its parts and honourable to the builder. Despite facing annihilation at the end of the 17th dynasty, with determination and persistence and with no concern for their own personal safety, the Egyptian monarchs acted to protect the people and preserve their coded way of life and succeeded in preserving a society which lasted for over 3,000 years but which towards the end of the 18th Dynasty was led to its slow downfall and ultimate destruction when despots were enabled to take control.

Today we look back on that great nation's achievements but have yet to realise that their extraordinary abilities in designing, constructing and erecting mighty structures many of which still remain today for us to admire was only a small part of their outstanding skills.

CHAPTER 1

Finding an Acceptable Approach to Life

From the earliest time it has been man's inclination to find the answer to life. Man has reasoned that there must be something more than the few fleeting years of existence on this planet and then nothing. Indeed the human mind finds it difficult, if not impossible, to accept that life does not have some further existence. Each generation, experiencing the loss of loved ones who have grown old and died, have been helped by the thought that they go to another, better life to which each will follow.

Religion in whatever form has provided a much needed comfort in times of stress to help us to comprehend the basis of life and the reasons why we must accept the changes that life brings, yet even today we still strive to understand the grand design of which human life is clearly only a small but perhaps more important part than we know. Science tells us that there is no after-life as we envisage it, in that we are only a mixture of chemicals which, when spent, will formulise with other chemicals to produce new life as in every other aspect of the cosmos, but, if that were so, it would be unnecessary for the grand design to produce creatures of reason and intelligence, the human race, and ensure that it survives and flourishes.

Of one thing we can be sure, and that is that logic commands what occurs in the cosmos. Each and every change has a mathematical calculation and an end result. If the human race was to be equated to a tree or a fish, as science would have us believe, there would have been no point in destruction of the dinosaurs in favour of intelligent beings with the ability to master the universe. Indeed, if one looks back on the history of this planet, an enormous effort has been made to ensure that man has succeeded against all the odds to dominate life on this planet, and, in seeking to understand the reason for this, man turned to religion which has sought to explain that there is a deity who guides and encourages us to achieve and that death is only a step towards our ultimate goal.

Clearly the human race still has a lot to learn, and in truth we have only just started to scratch the underside of the barrel of knowledge that the cosmos holds. Sadly modern religions do not have all the answers, and their efforts to satisfy intelligent man with explanations for disasters leaves much to be desired. But, when we need comfort, there has been no other satisfactory source, and we have had to accept that "God works in mysterious ways that we do not always understand" as the only explanation. We seek to know why our God allows people of hate and violence to dominate so much of our world and our lives, and there are few, if any, acceptable answers.

Throughout the ages men seeking power have so often made use of religion to persuade the people to accept that their particular belief is the only pathway to heaven and that it would please their particular deity to dominate others who have a different approach. Thus religion itself formulated for the benefit of man has occasionally become the encouragement to those who seek power to fall into ways of domination and destruction. Indeed throughout the ages religion, far from solving the problems of the human race, has been the cause of war and devastation. Extremism has continued to touch religion and produce a way of life among so many that has alarmed the world.

Horrified by this apparent impasse where preachers engender fear and hate and battle lines are consistently drawn, ordinary people in recent times have been attracted away from religion resulting in so many empty places of worship. As science produces new knowledge about the cosmos, new thinking has emerged which has taken on a surprising hold among all ages that a natural force exists throughout the universe that has formulated and guided and continues to guide our destiny. Indeed the attraction to a non-religious force that can be accepted by all mankind has an appeal to a significant proportion of the general public, although it is questionable whether it will ever surpass the fundamental reasoning that there is a living deity

Interestingly enough this new thinking was effectively reflected in the *Star Wars* theme of "good against evil", where "good" is represented by freedom of thought and from domination, and "evil" by the power of "the dark side". Man's ambition drives him to seek further knowledge, and it is conceded that this can lead to a lust for power. The problem has always been to so control the situation for the benefit and protection of all but without impairing man's passion for knowledge and improvement. In this respect religion has often failed and in some cases it has attracted and been unable to control those of evil intent who have led the people to commit crimes of the severest nature in the name of God, and in other cases has simply not provided the answers to satisfy and enlighten the lives of ordinary people.

This problem is not new. It has bedevilled man throughout the ages and has been and will continue to be a source of great concern that we have not found the right answer which will bring a measure of peace to society. As with so many difficult situations, we have tended to overlook the experience that earlier communities have had. We are so used to denigrating the efforts of societies and religions existing in the past and treating them with contempt simply because we think of ourselves as so much more advanced. Indeed we stylise them by referring to them by generic descriptions as heathens and people from the "Stone age" or the "Bronze age". Yet some societies in the ancient past thrived over many years without major conflicts and were advanced in so many ways, and much could be learned from the way they conducted their lives and their approach to death.

The tragedy that is portrayed by the history of this era is that having been so close to realising the perfect life, it all ended in disaster, brought about by a fear of change and a misunderstanding of the human quest for knowledge of the purpose of life.

This is the story of a community who had formulated a way of life acceptable to all it constituent parts. They had aimed for, and almost achieved, perfection in life but changed direction when its army took control. Yet, fortuitously, or perhaps be design, one man of outstanding perception and ability was able to improvise an escape for a tribe that had suffered enslavement at the hands of the new despot kings. That man was Moses who, with the aid of careful planning and a modicum of luck, led a vast number of enslaved people out of Egypt to forge them into a new nation built on the Code of Conduct that had served Egyptian society so well.

Like me, you may conclude that this plan could not have been achieved with out the help of a guiding power on whom Moses was able to rely and for whom he was willing to give up the opportunity of becoming the Egyptian monarch.

CHAPTER 2

Ma'at – The Code of Conduct

The ancient Egyptians had formed their society just over 6,000 years ago when their first King Narmer brought the lands of upper and lower Egypt together into one unit. This could not have been achieved without the support of all the people. This merged nation gave the people the advantage of size over neighbouring states which, of itself, provided some protection and the River Nile flooding the land twice a year providing ample food and water so the nation thrived.

However their success came as a direct result of the way in which they had chosen to conduct their lives by formulating a just and equitable society which the people supported and enjoyed. Contrary to popular belief ancient Egypt was not then a dictatorship; it was controlled by a triumvirate of whom the King was but one member, the other two being the Grand Vizier, the King's senior adviser, and the Chief Priest of the Temple of Amun.

Their religion to which modern man refers in the most derogatory way as "heathen" introduced many gods to govern each aspect of their lives during which they all accepted their role in the need to play their part in the improvement of their communities by using their ability and talent to their best advantage. Their ambition was satisfied by the opportunities provided to take on increased responsibilities, but their ultimate aim was to enter the "after-life" or as we describe it, the kingdom of heaven. They believed that this could only be realised by perfecting their existing life through a correct and acceptable approach to their deities, loyalty and service to authority and benefitting each other to which end they adopted a code of conduct which was analogous to their building programme and which they called "Ma'at" after the name of the Egyptian goddess of truth and justice.

The Goddess Ma'at

To become part of this closed society there was only one requirement; that the participant believed in a deity, a being greater than themselves to whom they owed homage, but there was no distinction made between the Gods of the various communities. There was no restriction placed on friendly foreigners joining their community, and they made no distinction in relation to their Gods who were also acceptable on the basis that belief in a superior being was the path to humility; an essential quality of a good life. In this way they felt that their existing life would be ameliorated and their transfer to the life to come assured.

It is logical to assume that their code of conduct was based on the concept of regard for others, charity for the poor and those who needed help, but with honesty being at all times an essential ingredient of behaviour. This would have followed their tripartite approach to life. Interestingly freemasons have adopted this approach as "brotherly love, relief and truth" and this movement is claimed to have emanated "anno lucis", in the year of masonic light, from a time a little more than 6,000 years ago. That society was open to all free men with whom they would feel at ease regardless of race, creed or colour, with the sole exclusion of slaves whose attitude to life could not then be trusted. Honour between men was paramount, so that there could exist a level of trust upon which a sound society could exist.

Egyptian society was based on equality. Neither difference nor distinction was made between men and women, creed or colour of skin; all had equal rights under the law. Subordination was accepted as a necessary adjunct to the smooth running of schemes, as someone had to take responsibility for decisions made to advance the project, but only those with the required abilities were selected for higher office or command thereby assuring for the recipient the respect of the community. Ma'at governed the way in which those who took command should behave and had become part of their way of life. Thus each individual from the king to the pauper had his place within their society; each knew that he or she would be treated justly and all were aware that there were punishments for those who overstepped the mark or used their superior rank for personal gain.

All were entitled to the basics of life; food and clothing, a home and medical and other support, but those of higher rank would receive additional wages paid through a weekly emolument to reflect the increased responsibilities of their work. Masonic history records the evidence of that procedure. To ensure that only those entitled would receive the appropriate level of wage, because there were no written certificates proving status, those of a higher rank were given passwords and signs which were used as a test before wages were paid. That ensured that each individual of that rank could take employment anywhere in the land at the same level of competence commensurate with their knowledge and ability.

Charity was a crucial part of their lives ensuring that no-one was overlooked in time of need. Although their medical knowledge was limited, anyone who was injured received the best available attention. Death and injury would affect the whole community, not only the immediate family, and the community took on the responsibility of ensuring that no-one suffered the loss of the necessaries of life. Although everyone worked for the good of the community, they were not without their human problems. They also had their difficult situations just as we have today. Exercising her equal rights in a petition for divorce, a copy of which remains for us to see in the Cairo Museum, a woman had submitted a complaint that her husband returned home drunk every evening. Some things never change.

Major projects such as the building of a city, a palace or pyramid called for the introduction of a very large number of workers and support staff. It is a misunderstanding that vast numbers of slaves were used for these major projects. Only the most menial of tasks were left to slaves as the Egyptians realised that there was a very high degree of expertise required in every aspect of the work if an important project was to be completed successfully. Because the Code of Conduct provided for a completely just and protective society, there was full co-operation on the advancement of the construction schemes and an enthusiasm in everyday life. This enabled their society to become the strongest and most vibrant nation introducing into their building schemes advanced technology and mathematical genius.

To achieve this end a substantial administration was required to oversee the erection of buildings of extraordinary design along with a major organisation of support staff used for providing food and housing, carrying water for those working in the heat of the day, washing, cleaning and medical services. These projects often took years to complete, and without an effective administration this would simply not have been possible. They brought this about by forming groups of 10 to which they gave nicknames, as we do today for football teams, with an appointed leader, and leaders of 10 teams and then 50 teams and so on, each leader rising to a higher rank or degree with that much greater responsibility.

At the top was the triumvirate; first with the Grand Vizier controlling the administration of the State, secondly with the Chief Priest of the Temple of Amun heading the religious side with the priests who, because of their learning and ability to read and write, also carried out the tasks of a Civil Service, and thirdly the King who was the conduit between the Gods and the people. They were the effective guiding force of the State which was protected by the standing army. Criminal acts against the people were considered as acts against the State and punished accordingly, but that aside it was recognised that every individual would carry out their allotted task regardless of seniority of office with tact and humility.

No-one was above the law with which all had to comply, and the King knew that, if Egypt suffered a serious problem such as a drought or an infestation of locusts, the people would assume that the Gods were annoyed with them and looked to the King to carry out his task of pacifying them. His situation was therefore as tenuous as that of anyone else in high office. All were liable to account to the society which they all served, and all relied upon the Gods to ensure that the State prospered.

All hoped that their good behaviour in this life would facilitate the transfer to the after-life and used their lives as a preparation to achieve that end. Their religion led them to believe that their bodies would be carried by a mythical boat along the Nile that took a course from Thebes directly towards the horizon where it joined with the Milky Way and that was the path that all would take at the close of their respective lives, towards the constellation of the Pleiades where the joy and pleasure of heaven awaited.

This journey would be broken by a number of gateways through which they would have to pass; each of which was guarded by a God who would pose a question to them about the lives they had led on Earth. If they answered correctly, the gate would open, and they would be permitted to continue their journey. If the answer they gave was wrong or untrue, they would not be permitted to proceed and they would not reach heaven to join their families and loved ones. All were concerned to succeed in this journey for which purpose they were encouraged to follow the course of Ma'at, the code that dominated their lives.

The final gate was guarded by Osiris, God of the Underworld who would weigh their hearts against a feather. If the heart weighed more than the feather, it would be thrown to waiting wild animals with devastating consequences for the deceased, but the reward for a successful end to their trials was a new life of true perfection with their loved ones.

Their kings were so obsessed with this concept that they put into effect their plans for the journey to "the stars" from the earliest practical moment which included the preparation of a special Book of the Dead provided at great expense by the priests to guide the king through the maze of gates instructing him about the answers he would need to give to the Gods and therefore the best chance of surviving the journey. The people endorsed this attitude towards their king to give him the best chance of pleading directly with the Gods for their safety and protection.

Ma'at provided the basis on which all lived their lives: the concern for others regardless of religion, creed or colour of skin; charity for those in need and truth, meaning honesty in all dealings and transactions for all of which there would be accountability. This scheme produced a standard of living acceptable to all, whatever degree of responsibility they had gained during their lives, and it is not surprising that this approach to life provided the basis for a peaceful existence which lasted for more than 3.000 years. But there came a time when Egypt fell into the hands of dictators, and Ma'at was replaced by the urge for power. It was then that pleasure was replaced by fear and dread. That occasion arose towards the end of the 18th Dynasty to which I refer later.

It was at that time that Moses endeavoured to carry the notion of Ma'at into the desert in the exodus with all those who longed for a return to those good days of peace and stability by providing a new improved religion of Judaism based on the principles of Ma'at but with the added advantage of a single unseen God. However, the escapees and their successors were to face endless antagonism from self-seeking despots which still rears its ugly head even today.

Freemasonry endeavours to emulate Ma'at by introducing a symbolical life akin to that experienced by those fortunate ancients, and to some degree this works today, as the masonic craft is still enjoyed by a significant number of dedicated individuals who, like the Egyptians of old, seek to experience an existence as close to perfection as man could devise. This produces so many advantages even today for Freemasons and non-Freemasons alike and keeps alive the possibility that at some time in the future we might be able to reintroduce the same style of existence for the benefit of the world as a whole.

CHAPTER 3

Evidence in Support

One of the difficulties in producing this history is that, prior to Julius Caesar in Roman times, there was no international calendar and little factual evidence of events. Snippets of information gathered from ancient texts or writings still in existence from Egypt or the Hittites give some guide. The Bible is also helpful but is open to some question in the way events are recorded.

Some of the information given is clearly reliable, but on so many occasions historians and academics have chosen to treat reference to the passing of a number of years as an estimate of time which they can replace with their own reassessment to fit their theories as to when certain events actually occurred. This has led to the question being raised as to whether such events actually occurred, particularly when texts refer to events supported by so-called miracles.

Examples are given as to the length of years that the Bible gives to the lives of people who existed in earlier ages. The obvious example that comes to mind is that of Methuselah who is said to have lived for 967 years, and indeed the ten generations mentioned that passed between the time of Noah and Abraham were all attributed lives of extraordinary length. Many have with some force questioned the record of such lengths of time offering suggestions as to the calculations being made in months rather than years or taking intricate percentages to explain the discrepancies.

All such conclusions whilst providing an acceptable result are unlikely as there would be no point in the authors of the Bible reacting in that way. What I believe is more likely is that the names given as individuals in certain cases were in fact families or tribes; one person following on from another, each of whom had taken the name of a leader. However, the average length of life may well have been greater in those days. In later, more stressful years the average span of life was to drop to 35 years. Terah is said to have lived for 210 years and his son, Abraham, for 175. It is hard for us to consider that people at that time lived for that number of years, but with the change in times this must be considered as a possibility. Even in the last 100 years the average length of life has been significantly extended no doubt due to easier conditions and increased medical knowledge, and we have today acceptance that we are living longer lives with insurers estimating that for the next generation the average expectation of life is likely to be in the region of 120 years. Perhaps with modern science that time will be extended further.

The individual who wrote the Book of Genesis wanted to record the lineage of Abraham from the time of Noah and to show the years that had passed since The Flood which came some 6,000 years beforehand when, due to global warming after the last ice age, the level of seas rose including the Mediterranean Sea, which spilled over into the basin that formed the Black Sea as we know it today. Names of individuals who lived during that period of time were unimportant to the story the Bible relates, but the lineage of the salient characters was fundamental to the book that was to form the basis of religious belief for the greatest percentage of people in our modern communities.

Indeed the recording of time in the Bible in other respects has also been the subject of question and dispute.

Where the author wishes to intimate a great length of time the period of 40 years appears to have been chosen by the authors. The obvious example of this is the reference to the Children of Israel wandering in the desert for 40 years. It is most unlikely that this occurred over such an exact time, but it may well have been necessary to have waited until a new generation had grown up before it would have been possible to enter the "Promised Land" for which a well-organised army would have been necessary which would not have been possible with those who had been enslaved.

The period of 40 years appears to have been a favoured length of time when expressing or describing a lengthy religious or special event. If one includes the New Testament, there is a mention of this period no less than 149 times. The number 40 appears to symbolise a period of testing, trial or probation. The Bible intimates that Moses lived in Egypt for 40 years prior to his escape to Midian and 40 years in the desert. He was also on Mount Sinai for 40 days and nights, and on two separate occasions (Exodus Ch.24 v.18 and Ch.34 vs.1-28), receiving God's laws. He also sent spies who searched out the "Promised Land" for 40 days, (Numbers Ch.13 vs.25 and Ch.14 v.34).

Here the Bible suggests that the Children of Israel who had heard the uninviting report from the spies that this "land of milk and honey" was guarded by men of mighty stature recoiled from any suggestion of taking on the inhabitants of Canaan and were to be punished by having to stay wandering in the desert for a year for every day the spies spent searching the land of Canaan, a period of 40 days. The fact remains that they were not then an effective fighting force and would have had to wait for their children to mature before they were in a position to make that advance.

Whether it was exactly that time is questionable, but other evidence alluded to in later chapters does give support to the fact that approximately 40 years would be a reasonable estimate of that period of time.

The number 40 can also be said to represent a generation of man. Because of their sins after leaving Egypt in failing to give up other deities, God said that the generation of Israelites who escaped Egyptian bondage would not be allowed to enter the land of their inheritance in Canaan (Deuteronomy 1), and they were to be punished for disobedience of God's laws by having to wander in the wilderness for 40 years before a new generation was allowed to possess the "Promised Land". This is no doubt an excuse for not advancing the movement into the land until they had secured an army well enough trained, to bring about a successful campaign.

Clearly the period of 40 referred to in the Bible whether days or years is not intended to be an accurate intimation of the passage of time and is more descriptive of a period of trial, and accordingly cannot be relied on for the pinpointing of important events. But the Bible was not intended as an accurate record of the history of events, and it has to be accepted that its sole purpose was to establish the salient facts and history of the Israelites in the formation of a new nation founded on the excellences of the principles upon which ancient Egypt was formulated qualified by the establishment of a single, unseen God.

There are, therefore, few guides in the Bible upon which there can be any reliance in the dating of important events, even though it would appear there could be little, if any, realistic objection to the fact that such events did take place. However, some time spans have to be reasonably accurate, and the first of these relates to the length of time that the

Children of Israel were in "a foreign land that was not their own". Genesis Ch.15 v.13 states that they were warned this would be 400 years and which ultimately turned out to be 430 years as evidenced by Exodus Ch.12 v.40. There has been some controversy over the meaning of the sojourn in a foreign land and therefore as to when this period of time might have started. This is crucial if this statement is to evidence the date of the Exodus from Egypt. Most academics seem to accept that this period commenced from the time when Abraham left the City of Ur in the Chaldees to settle in the land of Canaan which was then under Egyptian control and where they stayed for roughly half of that time after which on invitation from the then King of Egypt they moved into the Land of Goshen remaining there for a similar period of time.

However, it has been difficult for historians to take the story further by matching the events in the Bible with the known facts from Egypt. I believe that this is due to the attempt to place the story in or around the 13th Dynasty which seems to me to be the wrong era, and I seek to show how the dates and times can and do equate with the history of ancient Egypt but in a later Dynasty and with only the slightest amendment to the facts already known.

The other guide in the Bible relates to the time that expired between the Exodus and fourth year of the reign of King Solomon in which he commenced the building of the first temple. The first Book of Kings (Ch.6 v.1) tells us that this was a period of 480 years. I am bound to say that even this has been the cause of some controversy, where for the last 2,500 years historians have been endeavouring to explain that the Pharaoh of the Exodus was Rameses 11. It is suggested that the figure of 480 years is simply a multiple of the estimate for each generation calculated on the basis that there were 12 generations between Moses and King Solomon where the authors of the Book of Kings have assumed that a generation was equivalent to 40 years. There are some who maintain that it was more likely that a generation at that time would have been nearer 30 years, and they claim that the true period of time should be considered as 360 years.

In my opinion this attitude is not only wrong but against all logic. The Book of Kings is most definite on 480 years. It does not give the figure as an estimate or a rough calculation which would have described the period of time as "about 500 years", and nor does it refer to any method of calculation. It is a clear indication of the exact number of years indicated by those whose knowledge should not be questioned if only because they were available to ascertain such a fact and record it at that time. There are no grounds to consider that the period of 480 years reflected anything other than the exact number of years.

We do have today the advantage of the greater knowledge of the dates of the relevant monarchs and this has led me to believe that, with information from the 17th and 18th Dynasties of ancient Egypt and from the Hittites, we can now place reasonably accurate dates on the events that led up to and which followed the Exodus. This also enables me to show the domestic, political and social events that brought about the attraction of the Children of Israel to Egypt and which eventually led to their enslavement along with the names of the monarchs involved.

CHAPTER 4

The Start of a New Life

In about 1740 BC some time in the 13th Dynasty of ancient Egypt something prompted a substantial movement of peoples throughout the Middle East. It may well have had something to do with the effect of geological disturbances. The major volcanic eruption that destroyed most of the island of Santorini in the Adriatic Sea which took place at that time was so massive that it was heard right round the world, and this along with major earthquakes taking place at the same time may have had an effect over the production of food or drinking water which would have prompted or encouraged some to move and find new homes. Whatever the reason tribes known as the Hittites had emerged in Turkey, and were expanding into Greece, Lebanon and Syria and the Hyksos emanating from Asia had started to settle in the land of Canaan with some moving into the Delta region of Egypt.

The Bible tells us that Abram (later to be known as the patriarch Abraham) had been taken by his elderly father, Terah, from the City of Ur in the Chaldees, thought to be on the fertile land near the Persian Gulf, where the family had thrived over some generations as we are told in Genesis Ch.11 v.31 *"And Terah took Abram, his son, and Lot, the son of Haran, his son's son and Sarai, his daughter-in-law, his son, Abram's wife, and they went forth with them from Ur in the Chaldees to go into the land of Canaan, and they came to Haran and dwelt there."* The Bible does not give us any reason why Terah took this decision, particularly bearing in mind that he was not then a young man. It is known that Terah was 205 years old when the family arrived in Haran, so that there must have been some urgency to force the family to move home that quickly. Moving a very large family with their whole entourage and livestock must have been quite an undertaking and would not have been contemplated without good reason.

The possibility was that the movement of the Hyksos Tribe had prompted Terah to find a different location for the family. The Hyksos were a warlike tribe emanating from Asia and there would have been some measure of danger for the family during that migration. In addition, transferring their home to Haran, a place just north of the Land of Canaan in modern day Turkey took them away from the danger of contact with that marauding tribe, giving some safety for Terah during the closing years of his life.

In fact Abram, who on his father's death became head of the family, did not leave Haran until he was 75 years of age. By then the Hittites were advancing towards that part of the land and Abram decided that the family would be better served by moving on. Although his nephew, Lot, agreed to accompany him, the remainder of the family decided to remain there, and in later years, when Jacob made a special point of visiting there to find and make contact with his distant relatives, he was to meet the love of his life, Rachel, and her deceiving father.

The Hittites were a determined and uncompromising tribe, and their movement into the area would have been a very good reason why Abram needed to make urgent plans to vacate the area which that tribe were clearly determined to dominate. The family had animals on which they relied for their livelihood and, as north was a mountainous route and both east and west were blocked by other tribes, going south was their only choice.

Abram and his family realised that they needed to plan their journey with care due to the fact that there were many tribes in that whole area who would not take kindly to the intake of such a large influx of people, so they consulted with the leaders of the caravans travelling through Canaan from Egypt towards Damascus who would have provided Abram with some useful information as to the route to take and as to the fact that they were best advised to move as quickly as possible towards Egypt and to seek permission to settle in the southern part of the land of Canaan, which was their best chance of finding a suitable place in which to settle. Undoubtedly it would be a perilous journey, but they ascertained that, if they managed to reach Egypt, the king there was not averse to negotiations and might well be prepared to help them.

Meanwhile the Egyptians had accepted the Hyksos into their midst, and in due course permitted them to take official positions of importance in both the local and central authorities. Effectively the Hyksos would over time gain control of the Delta region which was to play an important part in Egyptian history. The Egyptians, perhaps a little naively at first, considered this mix of cultures to be advantageous. This was understandable, because the Hyksos had brought with them chariots and horses which the Egyptians had not previously seen, and they felt that they had a lot to learn from the Hyksos.

Abram with his whole entourage set out to travel through Canaan meeting up with a number of warlike tribes with whom he had to negotiate simply to pass through their land on the way to Egypt assuring them that it was not his intention to set up home there. There were many difficulties that had to be faced on their journey and bribes paid, but they succeeded in keeping their numbers and possessions together arriving at the border with Egypt. They needed to get out of Canaan because there was a famine there, an occurrence not uncommon in the Middle East at the time, but Abram was concerned about the reaction the Egyptians might have towards him and his family, no doubt due to the exaggerated stories that he had heard about them.

Abram decided that it was the lesser of two evils to chance his luck with Egypt, but told his wife, Sarai, that, when they met the King, she should be prepared to say that she was Abram's sister rather than his wife, as there was no telling what the King might do to take Sarai into his palace. Clearly Abram was fearful of the possibility that the King would want to keep Sarai, by all accounts a very beautiful woman, and, in order to get hold of her, might kill Abram (Genesis Ch.12 vs.11-14). We are told that Sarai agreed to this ruse, although there is no information as to whether she raised any objection. Perhaps she considered that this would have to be her contribution to the safety of the family.

The meeting took place with Abram requesting permission for him to settle with his family and entourage in the land of Canaan under the King's protection, and the King agreed to give consideration to the request. In answer to the King, Abram confirmed that Sarai was his sister, and, following his worst fears, she was then invited into the palace. The reply to Abram's request came sooner than he expected when the King summoned Abram and asked him why he did not tell the truth about his wife, Sarai. The King was clearly irritated and told Abram that he was embarrassed and upset that such a trick should have been played on him.

Abram apologised to the King and explained the fear that he had as a result of what he had been told about Egypt and the monarchy. The King appears to have accepted this explanation giving his permission for Abram and his family to settle in the land of Canaan in a specially chosen fertile part of the land and also gave him a substantial gift to express his regret over the misunderstanding (Genesis Ch.12 vs.18-20).

This was Abram's first introduction to the unusual code of living that was an integral part of the Egyptian way of life requiring all the people in the land including the King to respect the sanctity of marriage and to behave with humility and honesty towards others, and being mindful of his obligations and aware of the answers he would have to give in due course on his journey to the stars.

We know little of the kings of the 13th Dynasty which is when this event with Abraham and Sarai took place. The best information that we have is that there were over 50 of them who reigned over a period of about 125 years. It is clear that a very considerable immigration of Asiatic people did occur during that time into the Delta region of Egypt which was the cause of some concern to the Egyptians. Abram's friendly approach to the Egyptian king was probably seen as a refreshing change from the more aggressive attitude of the Hyksos.

Little is made of this in the Bible, but it clearly had a resounding effect on Abram who was, as a result of gifts from the King, by then very wealthy. When they reached the allotted place where they were to set up home, Abram and his nephew, Lot, had a discussion as to the future arrangements that they should make, and Lot decided that he would wish to take his side of the family and reside separately from Abram. Abram agreed that Lot should have the choice land for himself, and he selected the only fertile part, leaving Abraham with the rest. As the patriarch of the family and leader of the group in accepting Lot's decision, Abram had acted with a generosity far greater than would have been expected of him.

The changes brought about in the Middle East by the movement of peoples settled down. The Hyksos consolidated their control over the Delta region, and Egypt, always anxious to learn, was able to investigate the use of the chariot, the wheel, and the horse which they did not have before the coming of the Hyksos, turning them to good use in their protection in later years. At the same time the Hittites became very powerful in their chosen area and consolidated their position down as far as the town of Kadesh along the northern border of Canaan taking care not to infringe on the land over which Egypt ruled.

Abram and his nephew, Lot, built a whole new tribe called the Habiru which expanded into southern Canaan raising an army of warriors from their followers to protect them from marauding Asiatic gangs as was necessary if one was to survive in that area. That army would be a great asset to Egypt in the years to come.

The Bible informs us that God told Abram that his people were due to remain in foreign lands for a long time. *"Know of a surety that thy seed shall be a stranger in the land that is not theirs"* (Generis Ch.15 v.13). The same verse intimates that this would be their existence for a period of 400 years and end in servitude. In fact what actually happened is mentioned in Exodus Ch.12 v.40 *"Now the sojourning of the Children of Israel, who dwelt in Egypt, was four hundred and thirty years."* The land of Canaan was governed by Egypt, and it is not unreasonable to assume that 200 years of that time were to pass during which Abram, his son Isaac and grandson Jacob lived in comparative peace with their neighbours and where the family had become a respected institution in the area, and the remaining 230 years were spent in the Land of Goshen. There was a total of seven generations between Abraham and Moses with each generation lasting some 60 years. Bearing in mind the ages of the participants, this is feasible.

At the time Abram had achieved his goal. He had brought the whole family through a treacherous journey and was able to set up a new home for them in comparative safety with what appeared to have a sound base, and, although they were to be under the control of a foreign power, the people of the area seemed to be friendly enough, and he must have felt that he had provided as best he could for their future.

CHAPTER 5

Treachery

Nothing is for ever, and the happy and peaceful life in Egypt was due to be disrupted by one power-seeking individual whose name was to strike fear and loathing into the hearts of all Egyptians and put the ingenuity of a young king to the greatest test.

In the course of time it became clear that the Hyksos who, until this point in time, had maintained their allegiance to the Egyptian crown showed that they then had a different agenda and were intent upon taking over Egypt, and, when Seqenenre Tao II ascended the throne towards the end of the 17th Dynasty, they became unnecessarily aggressive. There had been a peaceful stand-off co-existence in Egypt over the previous 200 years and more, and the Hyksos felt that this showed a measure of weakness from which they might be able to take advantage. Insults were levied by local Hyksos rulers who gave themselves titles displaying an increased level of their own importance and the measure of their control over important areas of the realm. This was of concern, because, with a domestic policy of de-centralisation, some of the rulers of cities were maintaining and building their own armies.

One such insult to the monarch came in a written requirement from the ruler of their main city, Avaris, one by the name of Apepi (or Apophis as he is sometimes known), who pompously demanded that the King dispense with his hippopotamus pool, because "the noise of the beasts is disturbing my sleep". Bearing in mind the distance between Thebes and Avaris (about 400 miles) this attitude was at first considered only as posturing, and indeed today we would find it somewhat amusing, but it displayed a divided land with the Hyksos totally in control of the northern and Delta territories and a threat to the stability of Egypt.

The previous king, Seqenenre Tao I, had died suddenly when his son Seqenenre Tao II took control of the kingdom. Any change of king was always a time when the nation was at its weakest and this encouraged aggression from neighbours.

The people had enjoyed a pleasant and peaceful existence for so long and the last thing the new King wanted was war. But other problems were becoming apparent to the King's advisors who were warning the King of the growing infiltration into Egyptian land by the Hyksos who made little secret of the fact that they wanted to expand their influence and were showing contempt for the crown. It was equally worrying that they were also demanding to learn the secrets of the Egyptian procedures for king making. Previous Egyptian monarchs had been too weak to act against the Hyksos resulting in the loss of control of large swathes of Egyptian land. Taxes were not being paid, and, as the Hyksos got stronger with no reaction from the crown, the future of Egypt was in doubt. Clearly this advance had to be addressed. If the Hyksos were able to obtain possession of the secrets of king making, Egypt would be taken over and all would be lost.

Seqenenre Tao II still had an army, which, although dated, was feared by the aggressors. During his short four year reign, there were skirmishes with the Hyksos intending to send a message to them that the king would defend the realm and the Egyptian way of life. The Hyksos had a stronger and larger army than the Egyptians, but they wanted the secrets of king making. Believing that the king was then too weak to resist, Apepi sent men in an endeavour to force the King to give up those important secrets. They found a priest who for money was willing to provide information as to where they could find the King unguarded.

The skull of Seqenenre Tao II

Every day at noon the King, being a devoutly religious man, attended the temple to seek guidance from the Gods for his rule over the people and the assassins laid wait for him. As he left the temple, they surrounded the King and demanded of him the secrets they lacked. True to his obligations and despite threats to his life, the king refused to co-operate, and in exasperation they bludgeoned him to death. His skull showing the damage caused by Asiatic axes evidences the blows he received to both sides of his temple and the thrust to the centre of his skull that killed him.

Seqenenre Tao II was a highly respected and admired King. For an Egyptian he was tall being over six foot, but by all accounts a very gentle and genuine monarch who took great pride in his kingdom and his family and in his duties towards his subjects who had great love for him and were proud of him. He had desperately wanted to wrest the kingdom from the grasp of the Hyksos to the west and the advancing Kushites from Nubia in the south. Commendable as this was, the skirmishes that took place only served to irritate and encourage the aggression towards him.

This final act of violence against their King shocked the Egyptians, particularly as they had opened their land and their way of life to the Hyksos, and their betrayal sparked a wave of revulsion. Freemasonry seeks to recall that event giving great respect for that noble act of saving the people of Egypt from being taken over and protecting their code of living, establishing the principle of holding such selfless conduct in the highest esteem.

Sekenenre's eldest son, Kamose, was devastated by the loss of his father in this tragic way. It also meant that with his father's death the secrets of the inner working for king making were lost. Fortunately the priests who had investigated the felony had found the culprit who had led the murderers to their victim, and by using this story of treachery were able to prepare substituted procedures by which the new King could be crowned. It was proclaimed that this substituted procedure would be adopted until time or circumstances should restore the genuine secrets.

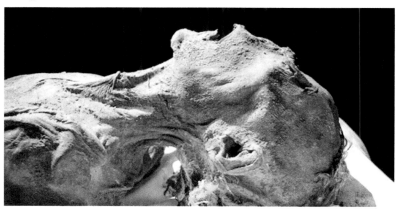

Image of mummified priest

The burial of the old king was accompanied by the punishment of the culprit who had perpetrated the crime to which end the faithless priest was "mummified" alive. His body was found close to that of the mummified remains of the king. Some have said that it looks as if he was screaming, but it is clear that he was gasping for his last breath as he suffered the punishment he so richly deserved.

Kamose immediately set about dealing with the problem created by the Hyksos and quickly opened a campaign for liberation of the stolen Egyptian lands with some measure of success. He had taken the army south to take back control of a fortress which had previously been meekly handed over to the Kushites earlier to avoid a fight. This was easily achieved which weakened the ability of those invaders. He then turned his mind to dealing with the Hyksos. He led his army to deal with the smaller towns which fell to his forces but sadly was unable to complete the task. His efforts did destroy a large part of their army which weakened the Hyksos significantly ensuring that they were not in a position to make an attack on Thebes, but he was killed before he had completed the task and, although it is not known how, it is most likely that he died in the course of these efforts.

CHAPTER 6

The Burden left for Ahmose

The death of King Kamose brought the 17th Dynasty of Kings to a close, and in the year 1539 BC his younger brother, Ahmose, acceded to the throne of Egypt. It was not expected that the monarchy would fall to him at all, let alone at such an early age, and this event called for careful handling. Fortunately the new King had the great advantage of his sister-in-law, Tetisheri, and his mother, Ahhotep, who took on the task of administering the land during his minority and organised his schooling. Both proved to be most able and hard working women and the people of Egypt believed in and supported a royal family who in times of emergency pulled together showing leadership of the highest quality.

King Ahmose was only three years old when his father was killed, and after his brother had died some two years later, he unexpectedly found himself King aged only five, but this was the start of the 18th Dynasty which would bring light and great fortune to this beleaguered State. Although the Hyksos still dominated the Delta region, this did not directly affect everyday life in Egypt, because they had the land adjacent to the Nile which provided ample food and water for the whole region, but it did adversely affect the stability of the realm because of the attitude and lack of co-operation of the Hyksos.

In addition the problem extended to the southern part of the kingdom. Sensing weakness in the Egyptian monarchy the

Kushites still had designs on possessing Egypt's southern territories. Together the Hyksos who also had close friends in Canaan on whom they could call in time of trouble and the Kushites were more than a match for the then Egyptian forces. The rulers in Egypt were only too well aware of the predicament which was exacerbated by the fact that spies had been captured by the Egyptian army carrying communications through the desert between the Hyksos and the Kushites which brought fear and worry to the establishment.

Some 10 years later in 1529 BC by the time Ahmose was 15, Egypt was ready to plan a campaign, but it would have to be one that could have some chance of success. During his youth and training Ahmose spent time in the army and also served on ships where he was able to investigate how he might build and train his forces into a more modern and competent fighting force.

He had learned military strategy and used it to the full. He had become personally involved in the modernisation of the army by upgrading their armaments and introducing the use of chariots and horses following the lead of the Hyksos which he had redesigned by enlarging the carriage to carry a driver and an archer, widening the wheel base to give it more stability and greater manoeuvrability and drawn by two horses instead of one for speed. Ahmose realised that the only way to succeed was through detailed planning and sound preparation and history has proved that he was right.

He knew that he would have to face an army larger than his, and he would need all his ingenuity to succeed. The changes he made provided the flexibility of cavalry working with ground forces which became an important part of his strategy and introducing new and effective tactics involving the use of ships. But he needed something extra to be sure of success: he knew that he would have one shot in this campaign and that there would be no second chance. Either he would be able to completely destroy the Hyksos for good, or Egypt would be lost.

It is all the more interesting that the Bible story of Joseph appears during this time. He had been sold into slavery by his brothers whom he had upset by suggesting that he had a close association with their one God to whom their great grandparent, Abram, had introduced them. On the best information available the event of Joseph entering Egypt took place during the reign of King Seqenenre Tao II in the year 1542 BC when Joseph was 17. This was during difficult times in Egypt and just before the murder of the King.

Joseph found himself employed as a slave in the house of Potiphar who was a Captain of the Guard in the army, a man of some consequence (Genesis Ch.39 v.1). It was not long before Joseph was able to prove his abilities becoming a useful member of the household, and in due course he was appointed head of the household. It may well be that the murder of the King was the cause of Captain Potiphar having to spend most of his time away from his home.

The Bible tells us that he needed an able and reliable individual to take charge of the household (Genesis Ch.39 v.4) from which we can gather that he did not have the trust in his wife to carry out that task. Joseph had been his servant for some three years and had proved himself to be a sound and reliable young man and the Captain considered that he would make a competent administrator. He was aware of his wife's shortcomings, but he was not expecting her to react in the way that she did. Joseph was loyal and efficient and the one upon whom the Captain relied to protect his property and his family in his absence.

The accession to the throne of a new King was always going to be a time of instability, and this would have been particularly so where the new King was so young. Although their enemies had been weakened, the Egyptians feared a further attack, and all those involved in the army would have been called to duty particularly someone with so senior an office as that of Captain Potiphar.

By all accounts Joseph was also a handsome young man and Potiphar's wife who had been without her husband for a long time began to take an interest in Joseph. He was aware of the seriousness of adultery with his employer's wife and rejected her. Sadly, after Joseph had been a loyal servant in that household for some nine years, Potiphar's wife falsely accused him of rape, and he was thrown into prison (Genesis Ch.39 v.20).

There he met two other accused men; Pharaoh's cup bearer and baker both of whom had dreams which Joseph was able to interpret advising the baker that he would be hanged and the cup bearer that he would be released (Genesis Ch.39 vs.21-22). This interpretation proved to be correct, and Joseph who was anxious to be released from prison and knowing that the cup bearer would return to his duties in the palace, asked him to remember this event and perhaps put in a good word to the King on his behalf.

The King's father and brother had been killed by the Hyksos, and he knew that they were preparing to make an attack, which would place Egypt in jeopardy and put his own future in doubt, and it is of little surprise that he was greatly troubled by his situation. By this time Ahmose who was then 21 needed to finalise his plans against the Hyksos if he was to save his realm from annihilation by them. He had gathered round him all the experts he could find to ensure that he had the best advice available, but this did not allay his fears.

If he followed his brother's tactics and led his army against the Kushites, this might be the excuse for the Hyksos to attack him from the rear. If he led the army against the Hyksos, the Kushites, although forced back into their own territory by the efforts of his brother, might break out and take the same action. Just as serious was the fact that, if he were to attack the Hyksos, their allies residing in Canaan would go for his flank. He could remain in Thebes for the time being, but at some time they would all attack and he could find himself surrounded. It was a desperate situation which seemed to have no answer.

This may well have been the cause of his interrupted sleep and vivid dreams which would have worried him, more particularly as he could find no-one to interpret them. What he needed was nothing short of a miracle for which he prayed but which seemed to elude him. Then something happened which was to give him the answer to the problems he faced, and this help was to come from an unusual and surprising source.

When Ahmose had a dream that could not be deciphered by his wise men, the cup bearer who had recalled the time when he and Joseph were in prison together recounted to the King the ability shown by Joseph in interpreting dreams, and he suggested to the King that it might be worth his while to see if Joseph could assist. Joseph had been in prison by this time for about three years by which time Ahmose had been on the throne for some 10 years. The King called for Joseph and was impressed with his interpretation. In fact Joseph went much further and sought to advise the King of the action he should take to resolve the problem he was about to face. He boldly stated that Egypt would have seven years of plenty during which time preparations should be made to store food in specially built silos, because the famine that was to follow would be for an equal length of time and would be very severe (Genesis Ch.41 vs.29-31).

Joseph was taking a chance because such effrontery could have been considered impertinence to the monarch who could have ordered his immediate death. But Joseph sensed in the King a state of confusion and serious concern and decided that giving strong and clear advice was the best step. He went further by setting out the procedure that the King should adopt and the process by which the King would be able to take total control of the situation.

This was the sign for which Ahmose had been waiting, and it is not surprising that Joseph's advice was received with some pleasure and relief. Joseph's ability and obvious administrative competence had impressed the King who wanted someone he felt he could trust to take charge of this project. Famines were not uncommon in the Middle East, and the Egyptians were fully aware of the consequences which would affect the whole area. If this was to take place, the King had been given time to make preparations which the Hyksos would be unlikely to do. He had checked on Joseph's abilities and knew from Captain Potiphar that he was unlikely to have committed the crime of which Joseph had been accused and that he was an efficient administrator. He seemed like the right person to oversee the arrangements for which purpose King Ahmose made him the Grand Vizier (Genesis Ch.41 vs.39-44) giving him absolute powers accountable only to the king personally...

So Joseph who was then 30 years of age (Genesis Ch.41 v.46) was renamed Zaphnath-Paaneah and given as his wife

Asenath, the daughter of Potiphera the Priest of the City of On (Genesis Ch.41 v.45) to ensure that no-one would suspect that he had made a foreigner and a mere slave the second most powerful man in the realm. Joseph made the arrangements to collect grain by way of a levy demanding one fifth of all that became available year by year, and with the help of the priests of the Temple of Amun built grain stores in all the major cities which by the end of the seven years were full to the point of overflowing.

As the famine started Joseph opened the stores on the order of the King to sell grain to all the Egyptians, first for cash and then for livestock, horses and other possessions and finally for property which secured for the crown all the wealth of the land (Genesis Ch.41 v.56). Only the land belonging to the temples was left to the priests to ensure their loyalty, because they were crucial to the plans of the King. But the people were fed when others in adjoining lands starved, and that secured their total loyalty as well.

Foreigners on the other hand did suffer. The land of Canaan was among them, and it was not long before Joseph's father, Jacob, sent to Egypt to buy food. When this was reported to the King, it was clear that his plans were coming to fruition. The Habiru of whom Jacob was one of their leaders were an effective fighting force, and part of the King's plan was to make use of them to secure the border between Egypt and Canaan. Thus arrangements were made for them to move home and reside in Goshen which was achieved with the promise of ample food supplies.

This would protect the border between the Hyksos in the Delta region and their allies in Canaan ensuring that any campaign by the Egyptian army against the Hyksos would not be interrupted by an attack on their flank. Two years into the famine Jacob who had taken on the new name of Israel along with all his family with a large contingent of Habiru warriors had moved into Goshen acting as a buffer zone for Egypt.

The Hyksos and the Kushites were suffering greatly from the famine and were weakened, and this ensured that the campaign so carefully prepared by the King would be successful. Nothing could now stand in the way of the well fed, re-equipped and revitalised Egyptian army. The King's strategy was to deal with the Hyksos first. Having cut off their supplies from Canaan he was able to take his army around their main city, Avaris, wiping out the minor towns and villages without any appreciable opposition and none escaped. He then turned his attention to their main city of Avaris which fell after three attacks by which events Ahmose provided his country with the return of the Delta region and a secure border to the north.

The King then turned his army south and routed the advancing Kushites who had ventured into Egypt in the hope of some gains and also dealt them a crushing blow in Nubia. By careful planning King Ahmose had recovered all the lost lands to Egypt's control providing a new start for his kingdom and a new hope for the future. At the end of his 25-year reign Egypt was once again the major power in the Middle East, but during that time Ahmose did not forget his domestic and administrative duties in his realm. He initiated a building programme to restore the temples and great buildings to their former glory along with the infrastructure of his country.

He also did not overlook the arts either, and with the Delta and Nubian regions once again secured under Egypt's control, access was gained to resources such as gold, silver and lapis lazuli. He opened limestone quarries and turquoise mines providing stone for monuments and negotiated trade deals with friendly neighbouring nations producing cedar wood from Lebanon and Minoan designs from the Aegean. He also started the art of glassmaking at first for jewellery but later used in astronomy and medicine.

His Pyramid was the last to be built in Egypt, although he was probably never buried there because of the fear of tomb robbers. It was not as grand as those of former kings, but its building had the effect of restoring the dignity of his people by showing that Egypt was once again a great nation and was psychologically a sound move.

Ahmose was undoubtedly one of the most successful kings of Egypt overcoming the many problems he had to face at the start of his reign and leaving his people a future of peace and stability. Although Egypt had experienced over the previous 250 years a creeping menace from foreign interference which nearly ended the nation, Ahmose had put his trust in new friends, the Habiru, later to be known as the Hebrews or Israelites, with whom Egypt would advance in every sphere of knowledge and life taking her to the greatest heights.

To his credit the King had not forgotten the Code of Conduct governed by the rule of Ma'at which secured equal rights for all including Joseph and his family then living in Egypt with so many others who had joined them. He acknowledged that he owed so much to the women in his life, his mother, Ahhotep, and his sister-in-law, Tetisheri, who had looked after the realm and provided for his education and the experts upon whom he had relied for advice during his early years.

Ma'at provided the sound base on which the future of his kingdom would rest, and it proved to be the greatest asset that

Egypt possessed. It gave the people the freedom they needed to build the economy and restore pride to their lives. There followed over 100 years of friendship and co-operation with the Habiru to their mutual advantage just as Ahmose had envisaged and all prospered.

Not all of the Habiru tribe had transferred to Egypt. There were a significant number who offered their services to other tribes living in Canaan who needed fighting men for their security, and others (possibly those who served Lot's family), and many found new homes in the hills of Judea. Their successors were to take an essential role in the plans for the escape from slavery some 200 years later.

CHAPTER 7

The Following years

Ahmose had masterminded a complete change in Egypt in the space of just a few years. He came to the throne in 1539 BC, a youth at the age of five facing the distinct possibility of Egypt's annihilation, and 29 years later on his death at the age of only 34 he had transformed the nation completely. Within that time he had routed and demolished the Hyksos and taken back the whole of the Delta region, a most fertile area of the land, and secured the whole of the south of the country from the Kushites so that Egypt had within the space of his reign once again become the most powerful nation in the Middle East. This was an amazing achievement for any man, but he was clearly a born leader of men with the great ability for effective, careful planning before embarking on any campaign during which time he had ensured the support of his newly found allies, the Habiru.

He had revitalised and re-equipped the army which with careful training and preparation had become a most efficient fighting machine. The three closest women in his life also played their most important roles with efficiency and zeal. Ahhotep, his mother, had taken on the responsibilities of administering the State with all the day to day responsibility that was so crucial, and, being a member of the royal family, she had the credentials to do so, whilst his sister-in-law, Tetisheri, looked after the royal household bringing up the children and seeing to their education. Ahmose honoured both of them by mention in stone in the temples which he was building transforming them into national figures of great importance. This honour was well deserved, as they had provided the stability sorely needed in a time of great stress.

On the death of Tetisheri and Ahhotep he was to show that he had not forgotten his wife, Ahmose-Nefertari, who had provided him with a son and from then was to be known by the special titles of The King's Daughter, The King's Sister, The King's Mother and The King's Great Wife. These titles were a sign of great honour bestowed on the wife who had stood by him throughout his rule and had given him comfort in times of stress and joy in the good times.

Ahmose had reopened the gold and silver mines and showered precious stones and gifts on his wife. Family life was important to the King who put himself and his family forward as a fine example for all his subjects to follow thereby strengthening the Code of Conduct that was Ma'at. Ahmose also encouraged the arts introducing glassmaking at first for decoration but which was later to find other invaluable uses.

Prior to his reign, Egypt had experienced 250 years of peace, but the leadership had become lazy and ineffectual which others saw as weakness, and, but for the outstanding ability of this young King, the country would have suffered annihilation by those who had become enemies within its borders. Ahmose was able to recover the greatness of Egypt which he managed to revitalise within the space of his reign. At the end of his life Egypt was once again the strongest nation in the Middle East, had concentrated wealth within the control of the crown, secured the priesthood and the Temple of Amun, introduced a massive building programme to restore buildings damaged by the lack of any maintenance in previous years and brought stability for the people and peace to the nation.

For the first time in over two centuries Egypt experienced a vitality which encouraged new business and investment, interest in education and science and an exciting future. Most importantly he ensured for that special lifestyle that had brought peace and prosperity for the Egyptian people, Ma'at, the Code of Conduct. This was to be a whole new beginning, and it is not surprising that history records his reign as the start of The New Kingdom, because that is exactly what it was. For such a young man to have achieved so much in so short a time was amazing and it is not surprising that he is considered to be one of the greatest monarchs in Egyptian history.

Ahmose never forgot the debt he owed to Joseph and his Habiru family whom he and all Egypt honoured with friendship and respect for many years.

Ahmose laid the foundations of a new era upon which future monarchs could build. He died at such an early age, as far as we know from natural causes, although life threatening diseases were rife at the time. But he had bequeathed for his people a new beginning, and they did not delay in taking up the opportunity afforded to them. Ahmose's son, Amenhotep I, became the King at a very young age, and once again the monarch was too young to take on the regal responsibilities. His mother who had received the additional title of God's Wife with which she was honoured by her husband lent her well tried and most able assistance, and Joseph, still the Grand Vizier, would serve the new King as loyally as he had his father. Thus there was some measure of continuity of governance in the land.

Amenhotep 1 ruled Egypt from 1514 BC until he died in 1493 BC and during those 21 years he and his entourage had set about restoring the majesty of the King and the royal family by instituting a massive new building programme. So much work needed to be carried out in restoring the temples and to ensuring the continued flow of necessary building materials. The limestone quarries were reopened, gangs of workers and stonemasons employed encouraging business entrepreneurs in every aspect of life, and Egypt flourished.

The royal family had the full support of the nation as they had introduced a new vitality into the lives of the people. Living conditions in the cities had become squalid with refuse left in the narrow streets which were in some places flooded with the rise and fall of the Nile, and that problem was at last being addressed with permission being given for the building of housing outside the city limits. This new benevolent attitude was received with acclamation, and with the priests of the Temple of Amun happy with the support that the building programme provided for them, it is not surprising that the monarchy was greatly honoured.

As with all monarchs the King had to make arrangements for his after-life which he did not wish to have disturbed by tomb robbers. He therefore created a new village for the workmen he employed to dig and formulate his tomb. They and all their families moved into new accommodation so that the secrets of the whereabouts of his place of eternal rest would die with them. It is interesting that, despite every effort of archaeologists, the resting place for this King has never been found. Amenhotep 1 left for posterity a special temple as a Place of Truth providing so much evidence of the life of the people of that era.

Sadly, no doubt in some measure brought about by intermarriage, Amenhotep 1 did not have any children and did not leave an heir to the throne. Realising the importance of a settled accession to the throne, Amenhotep adopted a man by the name of Thutmose who was one of his most trusted advisors. For the first time in three generations the new King came to the throne as a middle-aged man. The death of a strong King would always be a time of weakness for the nation which would remain so until the new monarch was appointed and installed which would take several months.

If the new King was a youth, it would encourage enemies of the State to consider taking some advantage of the situation. That is why it was to be of such benefit to Egypt that this new King arrived with a well-thought out plan for what due to his age could only be a comparatively short reign. Not everyone accepted his right to rule, but Ahmose-Nefertari, the well-respected wife of Ahmose, gave his leadership her support, and having had his royal status secured by a coronation and confirmation of his divine right to rule, issued a promise to take action against any enemies of the State that might still have designs of rebellion or insurgency.

He pursued his declared plan with vigour and determination. All recalled the rebellion of the Kushites who had joined the Hyksos in their attempt to destroy Egypt, and, as they had started to cause further trouble, Thutmose was determined to ensure that they were taught a lesson. Within a few months of his accession to the throne he took the army south demolishing Kushite authority over the whole of Nubia. He took his daughter, Hatshepsut, with him to instil into her the importance of strong leadership.

He followed that endeavour in the fourth year of his reign by a show of strength in the land of Canaan, first to ensure that the supply of materials to Egypt from that area was secured and secondly to meet aggression from the Hittites in, what is now, Turkey and Syria and from a new tribe introduced to the area from the east calling themselves the

Mittani. His fears that they were planning an insurgence from the place they occupied in what is now Jordan was imminent were proved to be true, and to meet this Thutmose made a surprise attack utterly destroying his new enemy, capturing horses and chariots as bounty.

Thutmose 1 remained on the throne for 12 years and by his death in 1481 BC he had secured for Egypt land stretching from the Saharan desert in the south to what we know today as Syria in the north. The surrounding powerful nations, the Hittites, the Mittani and Babylon as well as prospective enemies had been forced to respect those borders. They thought that they might have been able to gain some advantage with the advent of a new King, Thutmose 11, but they had not realised that the son of Thutmose 1 was as ruthless as his father when defending Egypt's rule of the land and the Egyptian way of life.

This was highlighted when the Kushites who were still smarting from their humiliating defeat by Thutmose 1 came out in open revolt and attacked and took over the fortresses set up by that king killing all in the garrison. They were to learn that this was an unwise move when the response was to kill every Kushite male who could be found including the whole of their army save their eldest prince who would be taken back to Thebes to be taught "the right approach to life".

This process was often adopted during those times to ensure that the people of the area were educated in the appropriate behaviour between neighbours and that they understood that an aggressive approach was unacceptable. It was hoped that the Prince would also learn the advantages of adopting the Code of Conduct and that on his eventual return to his native country he would thereby encourage peaceful trading between neighbours as a part of building a new regime.

CHAPTER 8

The ride to Great Power

When Thutmose II took the throne, he wanted to ensure that he should continue to advance control over the whole of the land and taking a tough line with any neighbours who would cause trouble, was a mark of his attitude.

But sadly, he was not to last for long as monarch, although he did succeed in achieving control of the whole area.

This King had been married to his half-sister, Hatshepsut, who considered herself more eligible to rule than her husband being the daughter of the First and Great Wife of her father, whereas her husband was only the son of a lesser wife. Fortuitously for her everything fell into place. Her husband had within three years of his accession to the throne established absolute power in the region for Egypt and then at a very young age fell ill to the point where he had become unable to hold the reins of power. Her stepson was to become Thutmose 111, but he was then only a baby which entitled her to act as regent. However, she felt that, as her father's daughter, she had the disposition and ability to rule, and she was determined to do so. Her position as the "God's Wife" gave her the necessary credibility, and she astutely manipulated her situation giving herself joint powers with her infant stepson. But there was no doubt in the minds of the people who was to be in charge.

Until that time the word Pharaoh would have been translated only as "great house" or "palace", but in laying the ground to prove her right to rule Hatshepsut took on kingly names one of which was "Pharaoh", and from that time on all monarchs of Egypt were known by that title. There were some who did raise the question as to whether a woman could successfully rule Egypt, firstly because the king making procedures were designed only for a man, and secondly as the accession of a woman to the throne might signify to prospective aggressors a weakened authority in the country and encourage attempted intrusions into the hard-won position of the most powerful nation in the region.

Hatshepsut was not to be discouraged. She pointed out that she was not the first woman to become involved in administering the State. The 12th Dynasty had seen Sobekneferu as monarch, and perhaps in times of the greatest pressure when Egypt was facing total annihilation Tetisheri, Ahhotep and Ahmose-Nefertari had taken the full responsibility of guiding the nation and leading the people with great effect forming the foundation for the re-establishment of Egyptian kingly rule and protection of their Code of Conduct. Hatshepsut saw herself as the embodiment of her father, Thutmose 1 and Ahmose before him, and with the support of her counsellors and personal friends one of whom might still have been Zaphnath-Paaneah (Joseph) she declared herself the ruler.

Whilst monarchs before her had concentrated on and succeeded in securing the boundaries of Egypt, Hatshepsut turned her mind to a building programme that would reflect the greatness of the nation and restore confidence and pride in the Egyptian people. She found a previously unknown architect, Senenmut, to design massive structures in a new and modernised style, erecting temples, palaces and walkways which are still today considered as outstanding designs. Obelisks were erected to record her total dedication to the important Gods, Amun, Ra and the Goddesses, Hathor and Mut (the wife of Amun and mother to Ra, the sun God, and to declare her love and admiration for the previous rulers of the 18th Dynasty and particularly her father.

Hatshepsut had not stopped there. She formed the Egyptian Navy with express direction to search out and find new places and peoples with whom to trade, and her boats sailed not only to all ports on the Mediterranean Sea but also along the Red Sea and beyond. Little knowledge survives today as to how far they travelled, but there is some evidence that they reached as far as South America introducing the indigenous population there to the method of building pyramids. We do know that they reached the previously unknown Land of Punt, although we have yet to find out exactly where that place was situated. Suffice it to say that this effort resulted in the people introducing massive new business ventures resulting in a sound economy, and with the Egyptians and the Habiru working closely together they had built a strong and vibrant community from which all had gained in wealth and pleasure.

Her reign was immensely successful and in some respects Hatshepsut must be considered one of, if not the greatest monarch who ever reigned in Egypt, but in the course of time, as her stepson matured, a dispute arose between them, as she was not keen to give up power, and he was anxious to take over from her. She had managed to hold on to power for some 15 years leaving her stepson, Thutmose 111 to take over as Pharaoh in 1458 BC.

She was one of very few women to have acceded to the throne of Egypt, all of whom had been successful to a greater or lesser extent despite the reservations of the establishment. Hatshepsut was probably the most excellent of all the female rulers. She oversaw a long and peaceful era and her building projects were prolific and outstanding to the point where future monarchs endeavoured to claim them as their own accomplishments.

Sadly, Senenmut who had been allowed some special privileges by the monarch whom he so faithfully served, disappeared immediately after her death. His closeness to Hatshepsut on an almost daily routine was the basis of rumours as to the relationship between them. Jealousies encouraged scurrilous suggestions that this commoner was behaving above his station in life, and graffiti of the most explicit sexual nature appeared on walls endangering his position. This was exacerbated by the fact that he never married. No-one knows what happened to him which is unfortunate because he was responsible for designing some of the most tantalising structures that exist in Egypt which fascinate even today.

Thutmose III found it frustrating waiting to take over the reins of power from his stepmother. Although technically it was a joint rule, from a practical point of view she remained in charge concentrating on her building projects. He was anxious to prove his ability to advance Egyptian control over the whole of the Middle East, but he had to bide his time in patience until Hatshepsut had passed on to her eternal life. In the meantime little notice had been taken of the activities of the Mittani on the eastern borders of the Land of Canaan who had been building an army and entering into coalitions with other neighbouring tribes ready for an incursion into Egyptian territory. They had built fortifications at Megiddo (described in the Bible as Armageddon) giving them complete control over the Jezreel Valley and the trading route through to the Jordan Valley and beyond.

This was a dangerous development for Egypt which Thutmose 111 knew he had to address. His failure to do so would have encouraged those tribes to make further incursions into Egyptian territory. But attacking Megiddo was fraught with difficulties because of the layout of the land and the fact that it would take about three weeks to get the army there at least half of which was through enemy territory, but he needed to take action. The Mittani took the view that with a new King, Egypt was in a weakened state, but they did not realise that Thutmose 111 was as good if not a better commander than his predecessors.

His grandfather, Thutmose 1, and the army had provided a severe warning to the Mittani to keep out of Egyptian affairs, but that was clearly not enough for them and they continued with their plans. Thus, the King had to take his army to meet the insurgents. A mountain range stood in the path of the Egyptian Army leaving the King the choice of three routes to reach their goal. Two of the routes would take him either side of the mountains, and he realised that both would be guarded by enemy forces who had undoubtedly laid traps for him.

It was for this reason that he decided on the third alternative which was a very narrow route through the mountains which, if the enemy had chosen to guard, would have left him unable to use his army effectively. This was a serious move for Thutmose, but he chose to take this route banking on the Mittani believing that he would not dare to take that risk. He knew that the Mittani were obliged to spread their forces over the two routes and that they would anyway need to leave some part of their army to defend their city. His surmise proved to be correct, and the mountain route was indeed not guarded by their enemy which enabled him to arrive at Megiddo ready for the fight against the city before the Mittani and their allies could return with the main part of their army from guarding the other two routes.

The sight of a strong and aggressive force from Egypt left the Mittani guarding the city in panic; they left their chariots and horses, dropped their arms and ran behind the defensive walls of Megiddo. After a long siege of the town it fell with the Egyptians returning home having crushed any possible resistance and with so much booty and many of the Mittani as slaves leaving an army post available to deal with any further trouble. This was just one of the incidents adding some of the greatest military conquests to the list of previous successes.

This enforced movement of a large number of people also had an added advantage for Egypt. Although many of the enemy would remain as slaves, there would be a significant number of the ruling and professional classes who would be taken for retraining. This immigration of different peoples with their customs and culture into mainland Egypt provided a truly cosmopolitan community. The influx and acceptance of immigrants was always the policy adopted by Egypt since the beginning of time and was very much encouraged by "Ma'at", their code of conduct. Marriage between foreigners and Egyptians was encouraged which assisted integration into a rejuvenated society. The foreigners took advantage of their new freedom and rose to great heights in business and professional life, to the advantage of all concerned, while the King added to the number of his wives and staff in his palace. The blending of cultures, trade and scientific acumen lent added stimulus to the economic health of the community and a blending of social interests.

Bearing in mind that this was only 100 years since the Hyksos had almost overrun Egypt, this was a totally different attitude, and, just as we have today with migration of peoples escaping war zones in Africa and the Middle East, there were those who raised concerns that Egypt was leaving herself open to such major social and demographic changes that her own distinct culture was evaporating in the clamour for wealth. As occurs in such circumstances this warning was ignored, and the King continued with his military operations, and receipt of gifts from all the surrounding nations. To counter any concerns expressed regarding his domestic policies the king concentrated on producing propaganda to mark his great achievements, leaving his subjects to focus on increasing their wealth.

One would think that such a society having enough good fortune for all who lived there would have been a place as near to perfection as man could devise. Unfortunately human reaction does not work that way. The wealthy seek more wealth, and the nobility seek more power. The King's officials became corrupt, and justice for the people was often hard to find. By the end of the reign of Thutmose 111 in 1426 BC Egypt had suffered a major change in which Ma'at had been replaced by a craving for wealth and power, and this also prompted a change in the royal family.

CHAPTER 9

Change for the Worse

It is not known why a change within the royal family took place. Amenhotep 11 had royal connections but was not next in line to the throne. By this time the king was all powerful, and this change was accepted, because Thutmose 111 had been so successful for Egypt throughout his reign that the people assumed the king knew what was best for them. The probability was that all in Egypt wanted the success story to continue unabated without the control of the Code of Conduct, and Amenhotep 11 was considered as the best man to achieve that end.

Hatshepsut had actively adhered to the old ways which had brought such success for the people, preserving for their protection "truth, justice and righteousness". Perhaps her stepson's enforced wait for control had left him with a determination to overlook what was at the root of Egyptian culture in favour of exercising his mastery in the field of battle. Clearly from his propaganda he considered that his achievements were the acme of his reign, and perhaps through lack of education and learning he could not appreciate that some achievements have only a limited life.

Amenhotep 11 started his 26-year rule by promoting all his childhood friends to situations of high places which he thought would secure his own position. This was bound to cause irritation amongst those who felt they had been overlooked, particularly where experience was replaced by amateurs and incompetents. It was not the Egyptian way and would not have been welcomed. This new King was clearly paranoid which was reflected in his ruthlessness in his military campaigns wiping out complete cities where he suspected attempts at revolt or secession. Nonetheless his reign ended peacefully and in the year 1400 BC passed on the rule of Egypt to his son Thutmose 1V.

Interestingly enough, this new King who reigned for only 10 years was a totally different character. He ruled in peace and harmony bringing prosperity for the people. The Mittani and Hittites had been receptive to a new diplomatic approach which governed the foreign policy the new King had adopted throughout his reign bringing trade agreements to replace military action. Indeed, he sealed the new relationship with the Mittani by taking as wife one of the daughters of their ruler. This confirmation of the gesture of peace brought new life to building projects and a return to the Code of Conduct. This king was also more concerned with home affairs than his father attaching more importance to a change in religious ideology stressing the importance of family life. After the disruption by former kings who had become despots, Thutmose 1V was a refreshing new start to the true Egyptian way of life.

Egypt had reached the zenith of her fortunes. No other monarch could ascend the throne knowing that they were totally secure without having to prepare for some military escapade to prove his ability to rule. The people were at peace with their neighbours and themselves and concentrated on construction of new buildings, and creating wealth and prosperity. At the end of his reign as he set out on his journey to the afterlife he had left for the people a legacy of perfection in life which we as the human race would never again achieve.

Freemasonry endeavours to symbolically relive that life which touched on godliness for those few fleeting years and still attracts the few who are prepared to make time to keep alight that small beacon that acts as a reminder of a life without fear or worry where peace and prosperity replace hate and corruption.

Sadly nothing in this life is forever and a rude awakening was to face the unsuspecting subjects of Egypt. Amenhotep 111 came to the throne in 1390 BC as an adolescent without a cause believing that it was crucial for him to prove his right to rule. There was no cause for him to take up and no reason for him to assert his authority on surrounding nations. At first he demonstrated his bravery by fighting and killing bulls for sport in the ring, as there were no enemies of the State attracting a skirmish by the army. He then turned his mind to how he could leave for posterity something special in his name by which the people might remember him.

The building projects that were produced in his name were undoubtedly remarkable, but so many were taken over from his father. He needed something completely different from that which Egypt had previously experienced for him to take his place among the great rulers. At first he achieved this with massive statues, temples, columns and walkways that marked his reign. But this was not enough, and he searched for a decision he could make which would single him out as a monarch to be remembered. Without war, disputes would arise among the people and quarrels between the various tribes were raised, and the King spent much of his time dealing with them. Sadly from the way in which he conducted matters it soon became known that his ability as a wise and understanding judge was strictly limited.

Left for prosperity are the Armana letters written on clay and retained in a special building housing the King's correspondence which show that there were many incidents that required a diplomatic approach particularly amongst his vassals. Perhaps it was that his patience was short that so often he chose to react harshly, and, when he was faced with a revolt amongst the workers in the gold mines of Nubia, he had it put down with far greater force than was necessary, which shocked the Egyptian people.

What is also likely was that he did not have the ability to come to terms with the necessity for the use of diplomacy in making decisions, believing that his hard-line reactions would produce a quick and effective resolution to a problem. He genuinely believed that this would be for the benefit of all concerned but did not appreciate that a decision based on a lack of true understanding of all facets of a dispute would have resounding effects on the whole future of the nation.

An example of this arose in a most significant event arising out of a problem that could not be recorded for fear of repercussions. The Habiru, later known as the Israelites, who had taken the advantages provided by a vibrant economy had increased in numbers and wealth. Whilst they enjoyed the company of so many Egyptian friends and business partners and contacts, they had kept very much within their own tribe with their own religious procedures and had not assimilated with the Egyptian people. They were a peaceful and friendly society complying in all respects with the law and dutifully paying their taxes and had shown only goodwill and friendship towards the Egyptian people with whom they got on well both socially and commercially. But they were nonetheless separated with their own unseen God and peculiar religion discouraging inter-marriage. Far worse from the point of view of the priests; their way of life with their one unseen God they called 'El Shaddai' had become an attraction to the Egyptians, and the priests felt that they were losing control of the people.

In fact the Egyptians had organised amongst themselves their own single unseen God whom they called "The Aten". As there is no evidence throughout their existence that Egyptians had experienced anything of this nature, it can only be assumed that they were becoming attracted to the idea through their friendship with the Habiru. So many deities created problems for the people, who could not even remember the names of the Gods to whom they wished to offer a prayer. Over the years the people had been introduced to over two hundred Gods, some national and some local, and seeing the Habiru so satisfied with their single deity it is understandable that this would hold interest for the Egyptians. Indeed there is evidence that Amenhotep 111 included his acknowledgement of The Aten with his obeisance to Amun-Ra.

This was reflected in a reducing interest in the Temples of Amun and fewer wealthy people were prepared to pay the priests to write for them a Book of the Dead to help them on their journey to the stars. This seriously affected the income for the priests who looked on the situation as dangerous, because the Egyptian religion was intended to be sacrosanct to the very existence of the State. The senior priest of the Temple of Amun reminded the King that only 150 years earlier the Hyksos had been the cause of a major disruption, and that it was only by stint of good fortune and powerful leadership at the time that Egypt had not been annihilated. It would be unwise to allow the Habiru to continue their treacherous behaviour unchecked, as there was no knowing what might be planned amongst their ranks as they were known to have initiative and ability. It would be better to "nip the problem in the bud" rather than allow it to build when it might get out of hand.

It was forgotten that it was the Habiru who had played such a crucial role in the saving of the Egyptian nation from the treasonous behaviour of the Hyksos; nor was the King advised that it was Joseph, one of the Habiru tribe, who had masterminded the procedures that had saved the nation from annihilation. Indeed this new situation was so different from that which Egypt faced in the reign of Ahmose. There was clear evidence of treachery by the Hyksos and none from the Habiru who had committed no crime nor shown any lack of loyalty towards the King or the nation. But the priests had their agenda, and the King was naïve and easily led into making a decision without thinking of the consequences.

The King did not properly investigate the complaint to see if there were any real grounds for taking action; he just assumed that it was appropriate to make a quick decision. He was not aware nor did he care that the situation had arisen because there were some who saw and were jealous of the prosperity enjoyed by the Habiru who were not sharing their wealth with the priests, as they did not attend temple services nor solicit their assistance in relation to the after-life. The Habiru had their own religion and their own leaders and did not feel inclined to interfere in the religious politics of the host nation. They did not consider that they should be involved, and it might have been considered as impertinent had they done so. But the priests needed a scapegoat, and the Habiru provided the perfect answer.

For the King a very simple fact emerged that there was a problem to be solved, and the fear engendered in the King by the priests as to what might result if he did not act with alacrity prompted him to make a decision quickly. He was persuaded that a failure to act on his part might end his reign with an unprecedented disaster taking from him all that had been achieved over the last 150 years.

Making trouble in good times is not an unusual phenomenon and a constant feature between competing vassal nations, but this was happening within the boundaries of the State and was much more difficult to resolve. The King decided to meet the problem head on, but this was to have resounding effects and shake Egypt to its very core. Amenhotep did not trouble to seek advice elsewhere before acting, and the priests probably realised that he was sufficiently naive to accept their complaint without any further evidence, and they pushed him into believing that he had no choice other than to act for his own protection, warning him that, if anything were to occur which might affect the people, they would place the blame on him.

It took little more effort to convince Amenhotep that there was an answer which would resolve the whole problem with the stroke of a quill pen. He agreed to a plan which he was persuaded was an answer to the whole dilemma and which would at the same time please the establishment and not have too great an effect on the extensive building programme that he had initiated.

The King had been advised that it was necessary to build two new store cities at Pithom and Pi-Ramese, and, as these were to be situated close to Goshen, he would arrange for the Habiru to carry out that task. So many of the Habiru had offered their services to the King in his building programme, as did the Egyptians, and some had risen to high office and had lent their expertise in the construction of some of the most complicated edifices, so that this decision at the time would not have seemed to be oppressive. In fact the plan was to separate the Habiru from the Egyptian workers, leaving it to the army to complete their isolation within these projects. The soldiers were left to control the workers and to begin to make life a little difficult for them.

The Habiru had done nothing wrong and had committed no offence, and the Code of Conduct simply did not permit punishment of innocent people. The King knew that he was expected to comply with the rules laid down by the Gods in the Code of Conduct. Ma'at was obligatory for all and the King ignored that Code at his peril. However, he felt that he had to please his advisers and find a way of reducing the size of the Habiru people without it becoming obvious that he was directly involved. Movement of workers between projects was a common occurrence, and this therefore did not attract any particular concern, and it was only when it became clear that isolation was the object that calls were made for an explanation.

The Bible tells us that "there arose up a new King over Egypt which knew not Joseph" who suggested to his people that the Habiru "are more and mightier than we" and that "we should deal wisely with them lest they multiply and join our enemies and fight against us." (Exodus Ch.1 vs. 8-10). Of course this speaks only from the point of view of the Habiru, and does not indicate what reaction the Egyptian people had to this new and questionable behaviour by the establishment. In fact there was little that they could do against the army, but this oppressive approach against people who had not committed any offence was unpopular and a worrying development. As in all such situations people were genuinely concerned what oppressive action the King might take next, and who might then be the object of his displeasure.

Amenhotep was encouraged to bring about greater control over the Habiru tribe, and this could be achieved to the satisfaction of the establishment by forcing them into service to the King and making that service harsh. The Habiru had nowhere to go to escape from this approach towards them. There was no escape, and they were at a loss to understand why this was happening. After all they had not done anything about which there could be a complaint; they had supported the King, working hard for the benefit of their families and the nation as a whole. This was to be the first episode of what was to become "a Jewish experience" to be suffered on so many occasions in future years, arising unexpectedly as a result of unpredictable circumstances.

Having secured what he considered as control over the situation the King then called in two of the Egyptian midwives who served the Habiru women whom he felt he could trust suggesting to them that they should see that the newly born boy children did not live (Exodus Ch 1. v 15). In that way, when the girls became of age and looked for husbands, they would find them among the Egyptian boys, and in the course of time complete assimilation would be achieved. In his naivety the King thought that would solve all the problems. It mattered little to him that this would engender fear among both the Habiru and the Egyptians alike, which would turn them against the establishment. Indeed, he did not even realise the enormity of his mistake and was even proud that he had succeeded in completing his plan without ostensibly attracting any trouble or adversely affecting the building programme.

However, he was not counting on the fact that the midwives simply would not carry out such an order and when asked by the king why his order had not been obeyed, made the excuse that the children were born before the midwives had arrived to assist (Exodus Ch 1 v 19). That was a brave attitude for them to take, as they knew that it would put their own lives at risk, and the Bible honours them specifically for that reason. This scuppered part of the King's plan which was a source of irritation to him leading him to direct that the army should see to it that all the newly born boy children should be killed and thrown into the river. Three or four times a year with some misgivings the army carried out the King's bidding, but the King's excuses for taking such action were considered as wholly inadequate and against all for which the people of Egypt stood.

The furore that followed amongst all the people was not easily assuaged. It was perhaps that the King was still a very young man and that it was clear that he had been completely misled by his advisers that the people did not take any further action, but it had a severe effect on the whole population, and there was a backlash which affected members of the royal family as well as the people that would see a major change from which Egypt would suffer greatly.

Amenhotep III reigned for over 37 years during which time he had carried out a building programme as great as any ruler of the nation both before and after him. His foreign policies were also considered as admirable in entering into treaties of friendship with so many surrounding nations assisting in arrangements for business expansion. He died quite suddenly of unknown causes before he had reached the age of 50. His reign was considered a success but for this unfortunate turn of events with the Habiru which was to have a reaction on the people in exactly the opposite way than had been intended and was to rear its ugly head when Egypt fell into the hands of the next King.

CHAPTER 10

Success Breeds Jealousy

Into this turmoil a young Habiru, Moses, was born to his mother, Jochebed, who was not prepared to meekly submit to having him killed. She had already given birth to a daughter, Myriam, and later, but some three years before Moses, to a son, Aaron, and this kingly edict to her and to all the Habiru people was a disaster. She had managed to hide this new child for some three months, but she knew that the soldiers would soon come, and she had to take some action in an attempt to save his life and give him a chance for the future.

So she placed him in a basket made of reeds that grew along the banks of the river and set him adrift on the Nile. She had her daughter, Myriam, follow the basket as it floated down the river. There were many large homes backing on to the river, and there was always the possibility that the baby would be found by wealthy and well-meaning Egyptian people, and the life of the child thereby saved. As luck would have it the basket became entangled in reeds at the edge of the river just where one of the royal Princesses lived. Myriam watched whilst the Princess and her ladies who were bathing at the time found her young brother. Then she presented herself to the Princess and offered to find a "wet-nurse" for the child, and this was accepted. Thus Moses' natural mother became involved in his upbringing.

There was no secret that the baby was an Habiru child, because he was wrapped in a cloth in the colours of the Habiru people, but this was of no concern to the Princess and her ladies who were not interested in politics and simply looked on the child as just another baby. If he was to be brought up in the Egyptian way, surely no problem would arise. Indeed it was not unknown for foreign individuals to be brought into the palace for training in the correct approach to life. Moses would be brought up in that way being schooled in the palace and trained in the army eventually becoming a useful member of the Egyptian elite.

The Bible at that point mentions no name for the Princess, but later information provided about a Princess Bithiah leads one to the conclusion that it was indeed her who adopted the baby child. She was one of the daughters of Amenhotep III and a sister to Akhenaten. She named him Mose which was a common enough Egyptian name meaning "drawn out" implying that he had come to her in answer to her prayers having been drawn out of the water. We know him as Moses, and there was no secret in royal circles that Princess Bithiah had adopted an Habiru child. She had never married, and it was accepted that she was a little unusual in character, but she was part of the royal family, and, if having a son kept her happy, no-one was going to interfere with her eccentricities.

For the family of Moses, this was a blessing. All of them were protected by their royal patronage from the harsher circumstances meted out to their people. Although she brought him up as her own son and lavished all luxuries on him, she acknowledged his natural mother whom she employed and gave free access to her house both to her and the whole family. Moses was schooled as a Prince in Egypt and all known knowledge was afforded to him.

There was a feeling amongst a proportion of the Egyptian priests and royal advisers that the Habiru people who were still looked upon as immigrants because they had remained segregated that they were receiving advantages to which the Egyptian people were not entitled. This would not have occurred if the Habiru had been assimilated into the population. The Egyptian commoners had to give part of their time to the State to assist in the national building programme, but so many of the Habiru appeared to be exempt from such obligations. The King was advised that this was a problem which the people of Egypt would consider as unfair and could be solved by arranging for the Habiru to become involved in national projects.

The excuse given about the proposal for these construction projects may well have arisen under the mistaken belief that the Habiru would be happy to be treated in the same way as their Egyptian counterparts. After all the Egyptians felt a measure of pride in completing the erection of the most complicated buildings, and the Habiru should feel the same way. Indeed such projects may have started out in that mode, but it did not take long for jealousies to rear their ugly head and for those who held more extremist views to become involved. The Habiru did not have the experience of organising projects of that nature and were not as efficient in carrying out such work. The army was brought in to manage the construction, and, in order to ensure that procedures were completed on time, the attitude shown to the Habiru people became rough and harsh, and it did not take long before the Habiru were being treated as slaves.

It is a lesson in life that where great success is achieved there is always someone who finds reason to raise fault and complaint whether through greed or jealousy or both. The people of Ancient Egypt were as susceptible then as we are today to these human reactions. Those who complained had no idea how their change in attitude towards the Habiru would end and probably did not care. Revenge was their intention, but the action they engendered would destroy the very basis upon which Egypt's success rested.

CHAPTER 11

A Nation in Turmoil

The monarch who should have followed Amenhotep 111 was his eldest son, Prince Thutmose, but he had died during the latter part of his father's life, and Amenhotep IV, the younger son, was suddenly thrust into power. He was not prepared for kingship and did not crave it. He would have been happy just to be a royal Prince without any responsibility, but, before he knew it, he had become Amenhotep IV. The year was 1353 BC, and he was due to reign for 17 years during which time he was to bring in his own ideas of the religious concept of the single unseen God which were tainted by what he had learned in his youth direct from the Habiru leading to the establishment eventually describing him as an heretic.

Inbreeding had left Amenhotep with an unusual body form. He had an elongated skull, a rounded torso giving him a feminine look and very long hands and feet. His odd look was considered by the people as the outward appearance of one who had the pure blood of the royal family, but with our greater medical knowledge today we know that it was Marfan Syndrome, possibly the result of generations of inbreeding causing weaknesses to both body and mind. He had married a sister, Nefertiti, by all accounts a beautiful woman, but one who had a forceful character and who would assist him to bring about mayhem. They meant well and genuinely believed that they were ameliorating all that was good in Egypt, but through naivety exacerbated an already delicate political situation.

Little is known of the youth of this new King. Moses had grown up with him in the palace. They had attended classes and played together in the palace grounds. All members of the royal family and those living in the palace who were not slaves were expected to attain a high level of education and would also have been trained in the army and expected to take leading roles in all aspects of life in Egypt. Educated together the young Prince and Moses would have been friends and shared life in the palace grounds. It is also probable that the young Prince Amenhotep made regular visits to the home of Princess Bithiah who had learned from the Habiru people about the single unseen deity and was herself taken with the concept.

It was there that Prince Amenhotep was introduced to the idea of an all-powerful God to whom one could pray to help in all cases of difficulties and with whom one could have a special religious relationship. In Egypt at the time there were more than 200 Gods, as well as all the local Gods relevant to the various towns and villages. People found it difficult to remember the names of the various deities, and had become attracted to the possibility of having a single all powerful God who would receive prayers on every subject of concern. At first the establishment felt that the concept would evaporate with the Habiru, but this hope died with the passing of Amenhotep 111 which happened very suddenly and without any known cause.

In the palace no secret was made of Moses' background. It would have been almost impossible for such a secret to have been kept as too many people knew about it. Princess Bithiah had not married, and, if she wanted to bring up a child, no objection was going to be raised particularly if that child was to be schooled and trained in the palace. It has been suggested that there was a prophecy that a male child would be born to Habiru parents who would become the saviour of the tribe and that this is why Amenhotep 111 had all the male children killed, but there is no evidence of such a prophecy.

The establishment knew the Habiru to be a gentle and inoffensive people who were stubborn enough to refuse to assimilate totally into the Egyptian way of life retaining their own deity and religious procedures, and with the increase in their numbers in Goshen this was considered to be a dangerous omen for the future.

The Habiru were still suffering from the effects of their isolation from normal Egyptian life, and the death of Amenhotep 111 gave them hope that their plight would be lifted and they would once again be able to enjoy the pleasure of living without the restrictions that were imposed on them. All knew of the friendship between Moses and the new King and felt that this might prompt a new approach and alleviate their plight. They had no wish to encourage major change in Egypt, because that might cause further difficulties and could end in them being expelled from Egypt or worse.

It was therefore with some concern when they learned of the intentions of the new King who was taken with the idea of a single God and was planning to depart from Egypt's traditional religion, directing all his energy to a new religious cult and the building of a new city to be called Armana dedicated to his vision of the unseen God they knew as the "Aten". This was too closely akin to their religion, and they realized that this would only exacerbate the already tense situation with the establishment in Egypt. Whilst the oppressive rules were indeed removed from the Habiru, they watched in dismay while the King appeared to direct his whole energy to this project.

It may well have been prompted by a significant percentage of the people of Egypt who had felt uncomfortable with the nature of the previous regime in ignoring Ma'at, but it was clear that the establishment would never accept such a major change in so short a time, and the Habiru feared what the future might bring for them, as there was no safety outside the boundaries of Egypt, only desert and brigands, and after 150 years of good living the Habiru were not prepared for that.

After five years of his reign, Amenhotep 1V changed his name to Akhenaten (the name means "follower of the God Aten") and directed the whole nation to worship only this new deity. It took him and his wife, Nefertiti whom he made joint ruler with him, only two years to build his new capital city, Armana, where he endeavoured to extol all the great advantages of his new religion, but despite every effort

Face of Akhenaton

made, the establishment remained firmly against his changes. This is not surprising because it left the priests of the Temple of Amun without the support to which they felt entitled from the monarch, and because it struck at the very heart of Egyptian life.

Just as important this major change had a severe effect on the priests who, apart from their religious duties, formed the civil service of the realm carrying out the tasks of ensuring that the decision of the Royal Court were put into effect for the benefit of the nation. They reacted by a lack of co-operation with official correspondence and disrupted all they could by delaying payment to the armed forces which they hoped would undermine procedures, but there was a limit to what they could do without incurring the wrath of the King.

There is so much of a misunderstanding about Akhenaton's religious fervour. He has been accused of treachery in damaging the establishment and ignoring foreign policy, and after his death a genuine attempt was made to delete his memory and any reference to his reign. The truth is that he did take an interest in his people and in foreign affairs as is shown from the many letters written on clay tablets to various rulers and to Egyptian outposts. He was a strong leader encouraging a unique style of art of the highest quality which he patronised endeavouring to guide Egypt to a higher ideal, but he did have his faults.

He was so taken with his new religion that he tended to forget some of the necessaries of life for his people. Many of the poorer classes suffered from lack of food and some chronic medical conditions brought about by the practice requirements of his new religious order. He also caused a rift between those who supported him in his new ideology and those who wanted to keep the status quo. For this reason the reign of the new King was considered by the establishment in Egypt as an absolute disaster and immediately after his death they referred to him as the heretic.

Possibly also because of his medical condition he appeared to be single-minded in relation to his religious fervour, and, like other members of his family, he was prone to rages. This resulted in him getting his own way, because even his closest confidants would hesitate to disagree with him fearing his extreme reactions. He had the power of life and death over all his subjects, and accordingly his orders were invariably obeyed. He would not listen to advice from the establishment that the religious policies he was adopting were the cause of a split among the people and could only have the effect of weakening the nation to the disadvantage of everyone. This was also bound to attract the notice of neighbouring nations which would bring more problems.

Akhenaten ignored the advice genuinely believing that his changes would bring only good to his people and pressed on with his plans regardless. He undoubtedly and unwisely did shift funding away from the traditional temples towards the building of his new capital of Armana for the worship of Aten. This caused great consternation among the establishment particularly as he concentrated on completing that project quickly with the declared intention of removing the priesthood of Amun from any power or control.

To ensure that the project was completed expeditiously he introduced with great effect a new method of building. Only the foundation stones of great structures were to be of substantial size and each of the remaining stones were to be small and light enough for one man to carry. In this way his temples and palaces were erected at great speed enabling him to put his new way of life into effect without any significant delay. He wanted to show his people that his new religion would be more in tune with their advanced way of life and that they had nothing to fear and everything to gain from this innovation.

Despite their initial concern as to possible retribution against them, the Habiru must have looked on this new King as a blessing, because he had lifted his father's edict of restrictions, which had caused such heartache for them. He had also lessened the burden on them of being forced to build the two store cities of Pithom and Pi-Ramese by Akhenaton's father, Amenhotep 111, but the undercurrent caused by these political moves would be meted out against the Habiru tenfold. The establishment considered that they were to blame for introducing the King to the notion of a single unseen God. They had also refused to change their way of life and assimilate completely into Egyptian society, making it clear that their intentions long term were against the best interests of Egypt.

For the time being, in order to ensure that there would be no disruption to his plans, Akhenaton brought onto his staff a young and enthusiastic army officer by the name of Horemheb appointing him head of his Secret Service with the task of routing out anyone who might openly rebel against the King's plans and to ensure that work for the building of the King's new City of Armana proceeded smoothly. Horemheb was a man looking for power and carried out his task with ruthless determination, but he also took the opportunity of getting to know the royal family and all the leaders of the various influential institutions with whom he ingratiated himself. He became very much a political figure who was determined to have a significant influence over the future of the nation. He served his King well and became respected, if not a little feared, among the nobility and officials of the palace. Most importantly he befriended the children of the King so that he could become their confidant and thereby set himself up to wield immense power in the highest circles for the future.

Most think that the cult of Aten was the worship of the sun God, Ra, because this deity is depicted by a circle with rays emanating from it. This concept, however, does not accord with Akhenaton's wish for a complete change from the worship of the traditional Gods in favour of a single, unseen deity. The "Aten" was referred to as the "mother and father of all that is" and was intended to depict a single all-encompassing God whose powers were unrestricted. This notion had great merit, but the method chosen to bring in such a fundamental change with such speed to a people who had every reason to maintain their long-standing traditions was questionable.

Akhenaton was a man with a single blinkered determination. He knew that he had little time to complete the task that he had set for himself to introduce into his realm an entirely new approach to life and felt that he had to act with all due speed. To this end he wanted to complete the building of his new City of Armana quickly to ensure that he could establish his new way of life with what he considered as an upgraded concept of Ma'at, the Egyptian code of conduct. With the change in the elements of construction he managed to complete the building of the main part of his city within the amazingly short period of two years.

Nefertiti had taken a leading role in this new religion and had encouraged Akhenaton in his endeavours, as it gave her the kind of power she craved. She also stepped in to assist the king with his foreign commitments and helped where diplomatic overtures were needed. In this she became an essential part of the monarchy.

Part of his strategy was to ensure that women should have their equal rights enshrined into everyday life to which end he appointed his main wife, Nefertiti, joint monarch with him giving her equal regal status, and he also provided her with her own temple. Previous monarchs had honoured their spouses by naming them "God's Wife", but this went a step further which led to a male backlash amongst those seriously opposed to this fundamental change in direction of the State.

The common thought is that Akhenaten had chosen the sun god, Ra, to be the object of his worship to the exclusion of their other Gods, but this was not so. It is a mistake to interpret the depiction of the Aten as the sun with its rays shining on his family as evidence of his worship of Ra. Indeed, the circle has no relevance to the sun, and it will be noticed that the lines which some commentators describe as "rays" point only downwards. Here Freemasonry establishes that the circle is the ultimate depiction of God being a continuous line without beginning or end, and the lines from the circle pointing downwards only and also depicting the hand of friendship are an intimation of the connection of heaven to earth and the connection of the Aten with man. This masonic concept may well have emanated from this time, and it is interesting that in generations that followed oaths taken on the "circle" were rarely broken.

After twelve years of their reign, Nefertiti suddenly died, leaving the king devastated. He was inconsolable, but worse, he ceased to discharge his kingly duties and for five years Egypt suffered from a total lack of any leadership. He did not answer requests for help from army outposts and nor did he attend to any daily business. He simply refused to become involved in the role of the monarch.

Akhenaten reigned for 17 years leaving behind him a divided nation and the despair of the establishment who spent the next 30 years and more endeavouring to wipe from history any hint of the existence of this strange king and his unseen deity. After watching his antics and those of his wife for so many years without seeing an end to what they considered as a fiasco, and realising that this could continue for many years to come, to avoid the Armana religious cult becoming completely entrenched in Egyptian society, the establishment became so incensed by his attitude that they determined to reverse the reforms he and Nefertiti had installed and they laid plans to effect this change as soon as possible But Akhenaten left for posterity a new approach to life that was to have resounding effects on the whole world. Nefertiti gave him only daughters, at least six in number, one of whom, Meritaten, was to take the throne on the death of her father jointly with Smenkara, Akhenaten's uncle and her great uncle whom she was required to marry.

Like all kings wanting to ensure the future of the dynasty Akhenaten had produced a son. It was at first thought that his second wife, Kiya, might have mothered Tutankhaten, but

Tut's natural mother was his father's fourth daughter who was the spitting image of her mother, Nefertiti. Akhenaten loved his wife and in his psychological condition, some two years after her death he had a relationship with his daughter, who was for him the embodiment of his beautiful wife. That relationship produced his son, Tutankhaten, who was to suffer an even worse medical condition than that of his father.

Akhenaten died three years later and as Tutankhaten was so young and following the tradition that the mother of the new king would be his regent, Meritaten would take the throne.

The powers in Egypt realised that this could cause trouble with the establishment, so they gave Meritaten the new name of Neferneferuaten and married her to her aged uncle, Smenkara by which ruse they hoped to settle the division in the community and control the political trouble caused by the last king. However, the problems were not to be so easily solved.

CHAPTER 12

Restoring the Equilibrium

At that time Egypt was controlled by three advisors who were the most powerful men in the realm namely, the Grand Vizier Ai, who may have been a member of the royal family, the head of the army, General Horemheb, who had gained his position under Akhenaten's rule, and Maya, the Overseer of the Treasury. They realised that it was crucial to change the direction of kingly leadership after what they considered to have been a dangerous period during the Armana regime and brought about this formulated joint accession of Meretaton, who they renamed Neferneferuaten with Smenkara which at least gave the necessary royal look to the arrangement and gave them the time to re-establish the administration of the realm.

This regime did not last for long, and probably only about four years in all. No records exist as to what activities or events took place during that time or how Neferneferuaten and Smenkara died. On the death of Akhenaten, Smenkara, who was probably in his eighties, only lived for about four years, leaving Neferneferuaten to hold power alone for the following three years. She may well have been more closely involved with the Armana regime of her parents than was good for her and even possibly endeavoured to interfere in the reform of the realm which might have brought about her premature demise.

It is a matter of significance that nothing of note happened during her short reign, and it is distinctly possible that the three advisors concluded that they should remove any further opposition to their plans and replace Neferneferuaten with Akhenaten's eldest son who was by then nine-years-old. At that age he was not old enough to take over leadership of the realm, but his youth meant that he could be kept under the control of the triumvirate who had taken command of the realm wielding all the kingly power.

Tutankhaten was crowned king before he had attained his 10th birthday. It was still deemed necessary at this time to have royalty on the throne, and his age did give the triumvirate certain advantages. However, like other members of his family, Tut had a violent temper and needed to be handled with great care and tact. Horemheb who had made a special point of befriending the young King during his youth and had also assisted in his army training prided himself that he was able to bring calm to his royal patron. As with all such circumstances Horemheb had his own scheme in mind about which the other members of the triumvirate then had no knowledge.

Tutankhaten, who was obviously no-one's fool, realised that, if he was to become king, he needed the support of those wielding power in the realm to which end, at their request, he agreed to change his name to Tutankhamun (blessed in life by the God Amon). He had been married to his sister, Ankhesenamun, and from all accounts they were a very happy and young married couple. Sadly, things did not work out as he had planned. He was the last of his dynasty, and he needed children, and particularly a son, if the royal family was to be secured, but his wife had only given birth to two still-born children.

King Tutankhamun suffered from serious medical problems, like his father but worse, and so many of these were the result of a long line of inter-marriage. He had the family traits of a distorted body, but worse he had two club feet which made it very difficult for him to stand for any length of time or walk even with the aid of two sticks. He suffered from diabetes, and from the most severe form of malaria, and it is believed possibly also from sickle cell disease. To add to his discomfort he may well have had problems with his teeth all of which left him in constant pain. His life was undoubtedly a trial in itself, and it is not surprising that he suffered from a short temper.

Horemheb was not slow to realise that the King's disabilities were unlikely to allow him to produce an heir, and he had managed to persuade him that Egypt needed strong leadership for the safety of the realm, and that, if anything were to happen to the King, only he, Horemheb, could provide this. The King had a duty to ensure for the future of Egypt which could only be achieved by the appointment of him as "Lord of the Land". Whether or not Tut realised that this was the culmination of Horemheb's agenda, Tut had agreed to this arrangement for the sake of the stability of his realm by which appointment Horemheb at once secured his future as the next hereditary Pharaoh with the immediate power to create new laws.

Tut had tried to take a leading role as King, but his medical condition had made that very difficult. He did lead the army towards a skirmish against the Mittani tribe at the beginning of his reign, but it is unlikely that he took any direct part in the battle. General Horemheb wanted to give him the opportunity of showing that he was capable of discharging the duties of a king, and no doubt as part of his method of ingratiating himself with the monarch on whom he relied to ensure that he would be the next in line. Horemheb could afford to bide his time; he had the army behind him, and there was no-one in line to the throne who could challenge him. In the meantime he had control of the State and was making all the decisions in the name of the King.

Tut remained king for nearly 10 years during which time the three advisors restored the main deities of the realm headed by the father of all the Gods, Amun, and this ended the formal worship of the Aten. The city of Armana was taken apart stone by stone and the capital of the realm moved back to Thebes. Building projects were once again initiated in both Thebes and Karnak dedicating a new Temple to Amun. Many monuments were erected, and traditional festivals celebrated once again.

There are no records of how King Tut died. There is some speculation that he was assassinated, but that is unlikely, because there would have been no reason for anyone to cause his premature death, and not even Horemheb would have dared to take that course of action, as it would have placed a question over his own accession to the throne. As a young man Tut loved speed, and Horemheb arranged to have built for him a special chariot drawn by two strong horses by which the skilful rider could reach speeds of up to 40 mph. The vehicle had to be very light in weight, so that great ability was required to keep it on an even keel. It is more likely that, in racing his chariot in the desert, it hit a rock throwing its rider to the ground. As a young man there is little doubt that Tut was an accomplished chariot driver, but he had the disadvantage of two club feet, and the accident easily threw him off balance.

He ended up from this accident on his back on the ground with a chariot wheel riding over his torso. This fall also resulted in a small crack to the back of his skull and a clean break of his right femur just above the knee. Under normal circumstances this incident would not have been life threatening, but his medical condition arising from congenital defects that are manifest among children of incestuous relationships, the totality of which might well have weakened him and brought an early end to his life. His return to the palace at Thebes must have been extremely painful for him, and it is probable that, in the delay that had been occasioned by his slow journey, his leg had become infected and that his death was actually caused by septicaemia.

Ankhesenamun was left a very young widow of about 18 years of age and was therefore vulnerable. Whatever she did would be watched closely by the triumvirate. Egypt without a monarch would be considered by neighbouring tribes as weak and vulnerable to attack. Protection of the nation was paramount and required strong leadership to secure its people and its borders. It would be several months before a new king could be chosen, and during that time Horemheb would have immediately taken the army to patrol the borders of the nation and to deal with any hopeful aggressors.

CHAPTER 13

A Disaster Looming

Tut's death was followed by a political tussle for the crown between Horemheb who controlled the army, and the Grand Vizier, Ai. Although Horemheb had secured the office of Lord of the Land, Ai had the advantage of being a member of the royal family. This created some dilemma which would need a political and diplomatic solution of some kind. One result was clear that Ankhesenamun was left in the invidious situation of being in the way of powerful men, and she had become desperate.

She realised that her life was in danger and that she would have to be removed one way or another and she searched for a method of protecting her position. Without taking any advice from anyone with political knowledge she decided that she needed to find someone suitable to marry and wrote to the King of the Hittites, Suppiliumas, asking him to send one of his nine sons to marry her and to share the throne of Egypt with her. Clearly, she did not appreciate the enormity of her error. Whilst Suppiliumas may well have had some sympathy for her predicament, the letter had placed him in a most invidious position. He did not answer because this might well have been a trap for him, and it did not suit his purposes at the time to enter into a war with his powerful neighbours.

When he failed to reply to Ankhesenamun, she became even more concerned as to her position and wrote again begging him for assistance, and on this occasion he did reply. Perhaps he took pity on her realising her personal plight, although it is more likely that he was aware that the Egyptians were without any royal succession to the throne and felt that there was a chance of expanding his own empire without a conflict. If he did assume that this arrangement might have been acceptable to the Egyptians, he had misread the situation badly.

Suppiliumas had prepared one of his sons to travel to Egypt with a suitable entourage, but sadly for him and Ankhesenamun the Prince was murdered when he entered the land of Canaan. There was no love lost between the two states, and the possibility was that the Prince had run into a patrol of the Egyptian army, and Horemheb had made the assumption that this was a disguised attempt at aggression. In any event the effort of extending the attachment of Ankhesenamun to the throne was not on his agenda. With the murder of the Hittite Prince, Ankhesenamun lost her last hope of a happy future, and she became resigned to her fate.

By this time Horemheb had become obsessive about returning Egypt to the traditional Gods and was threatening to take extreme action to restore law and order. Grand Vizier Ai realised that the accession of Horemheb to the throne of Egypt would be a catastrophe for the nation and her people and he had hoped for the opportunity to intervene, and the action taken by the Queen gave him the opening he needed. Clearly her approach to the King of the Hittites was a treasonable act, particularly as she had offered to share the Egyptian throne with a member of the royal family of one of Egypt's enemies. On Horemheb's return this error was bound to give him the opportunity of arranging for her to face a public trial with an obvious and uncomfortable result. Ai approached her to explain that he had a plan by which she could be saved by a simple agreement for her to marry him. This would achieve what they both wanted, namely the opportunity for him to become the next Pharaoh and to exclude Horemheb, and at the same time it would save her from a certain and unpleasant death and also give her the opportunity of remaining as Queen.

It could not have been very palatable for Ankhesenamun to have been faced with a marriage to someone who was old enough to be her grandfather, but her death for treason was an even less palatable alternative. By this simple ruse Grand Vizier Ai achieved the political advantage, as he would marry Ankhesenamun before Horemheb returned to Thebes and present him with a *"fait accompli"*.

Thus, in 1322 BC, Grand Vizier Ai acceded to the throne in place of Horemheb, but he only survived four years. He had tried to exclude Horemheb by appointing his own son, Nakhtmin, to succeed him, but this simply incensed Horemheb who was not to be deflected by this trickery from what he considered to be his lawful right, and, after Ai had died in 1319 BC, he seized power and nothing more was heard of Ankhesenamun or Nakhtmin.

With no opposition left who were prepared to take on the army, Horemheb became the next Pharaoh and took on absolute dictatorial powers. His reign was to last for some 27 years, but he was to leave a trail of destruction and despair which brought a sad close to the 18th Dynasty. Ai had realised only too late that Horemheb whose whole life had been the army simply lacked the learning, finesse and diplomatic abilities necessary for kingship. Although he had spent time in the palace, he had not been taught the approach needed for political leadership which had been instilled into the minds of all in the royal family. His only concept of leadership was total and absolute control by order and restrictions in every aspect of life, and his approach reflected his army training.

The Armana cult and the vast changes to the lives of the people made by Akhenaten had brought turmoil to the country and the people were having to face the consequences of the chaos brought about by yet more changes to their daily lives. Efforts had been made to gently persuade the people to revert to the former Egyptian gods, but by this time a significant percentage of the population had adopted the cult of Aten as their preferred religion with a divisive effect on the nation. The government had failed to control the people by persuasion, and Horemheb felt that by bringing in more stringent directives with increased taxation to pay for restorative works and greater workloads for the workers it would force a uniformity considered by Horemheb as a necessary adjunct to a reformed state.

To ensure that any reference to the Armana regime was buried for good, Horemheb insisted on a massive building programme taking apart the city of Armana, deleting all references to the Aten cult, and removing the names of the rulers Akhenaten, Smenkara and Neferneferuaten depicted on any monuments of the whole of that family including, no doubt out of spite, those mentioning Tutankhamun and Ai. In this way Horemheb felt that they would be obliterated from history and thus from the minds of the people furthering his task of restoring Egypt once again to her full glory.

Horemheb was born a commoner and rose to political heights through the army. Egypt had accepted Pharaohs before who were not of the immediate royal family, but they were either distant members of the royal family or had some understanding of leadership or some sense of nobility and had understood that the strength of Egypt lay in Ma'at, the Code of Conduct, which bound the people together to work as a team and to live in peace and harmony with one another. Horemheb knew only how to give and take orders and thought that success in his endeavours would be established in this way.

Pharaoh Ai, realising the consequences for the people and the nation of allowing such a despot to take power, schemed to arrest Egypt from his grasp. Sadly his efforts were too late, and he could only keep Horemheb from the throne for a few years. Thus a merciless dictator ascended the throne of Egypt bringing his brand of rough order and strict control to a land that in earlier years had formulated a more gentle approach to life.

As with all such dictators, to avoid having to face any pointed questions, he needed a scapegoat, and what better section of the community could be found than the Israelites. They had grown numerous and wealthy living a comfortable life with, and, as Horemheb would have put it, "at the expense" of the Egyptian people. This was to result in their enslavement as enemies of the State which prompted them to take on the new name of Israelites in honour of their respected predecessor, Jacob, who had been renamed Israel, to signify their longing to leave Egypt as in death he had done and to found their own nation.

But the Egyptian people were to suffer as well. Despite Horemheb's endeavours to place the blame for his strict regime on his scapegoats, his fanatical fear of opposition led him to turn neighbour against neighbour and brother against brother encouraging reports of any possible "treasonable activities" in seeking out those who might still honour the then offending deity of The Aten or mention of any possible thought of insurrection. Egypt now entered a time when no-one was safe and all lived in fear of reprisals.

CHAPTER 14

Dictatorship Results

During his time at the palace since being appointed by Akhenaten to provide security for the Crown Horemheb had seen a level of corruption and mismanagement that had gone unchecked. Over the years so many well-placed individuals had made personal fortunes at the expense of the country and the people, and this had been something of concern for him. He had also watched decisions being made by the courts which were clearly intended to give advantages to well-placed individuals, and he had resolved that this would attract his first attention.

Resolving these problems would clearly be popular with the people, and it suited his purpose to make fundamental changes which would, at least on the face of it, bring justice to the nation. It may well have been that corruption was rife in the land and that the wealthy did pay bribes, but whether the problem was as serious or wide spread as he made out is questionable. The fact was that he made this the excuse to appoint new judges to the courts from the ranks of the army and to bring in harsh new laws against corrupt behaviour.

This method of control spread also to the palace where all his staff came under the strict military style protocols that also provided for bonuses to be paid for loyal service to the King. As he had planned at the commencement of his reign, this led to Horemheb being styled as a good and vigilant ruler and he was applauded for his "good deeds". In this way he claimed to have brought a measure of certainty to a land that had suffered from decades of political upheaval; bringing honesty to the commercial world and justice to the people.

The Israelites who had gained so much from the Egyptian people in knowledge and wealth had undoubtedly supported and would have outwardly encouraged the Armana project and in Horemheb's eyes would have deserved to pay for their "treachery". It may have been that there were some Israelites who had been involved in some of the misbehaviour, but paying bribes had become the only way to do business and their behaviour was no worse than those who insisted on receiving the bribes. In Horemheb's eyes there could have been no better reason for enslavement of the whole tribe and the best excuse for putting them under the lash. In this way he achieved his dual aims; to obliterate all references to the former regimes and to demolish any recognition of the single God, whilst at the same time rebuilding the old establishment to his own glory.

In Horemheb's mind there was also another advantage in taking action against the Israelites in that they had become too powerful. They had inveigled their way into Egyptian society and pretended to befriend the people and his paranoia led him to the conclusion that they had a similar agenda to that of the Hyksos and were putting into effect their plans to take over the nation. This was evidenced by their introduction of the single unseen god which so many of the Egyptian people had been naive enough to have adopted. Akhenaten had been fooled into thinking that this was innocent, and he did not realise that the Israelites could not and should not be trusted. With this excuse he could take the wealth of the people and use it for re-establishing the greatness that was Egypt.

As a warning to the world and particularly to the people of Egypt, the Israelites would pay the price for daring to challenge the greatest power on earth. But, as all dictators have to learn at some time, it is never possible to erase an ideology, particularly a religious fervour, by vicious and uncompromising acts of hate. It was patently obvious to the people of Egypt that this attitude was based on a lie, but against the determination of the King who was supported by the army they could do nothing about it. The rulings from this uncompromising dictator simply drove the new religion underground, and the more repressive the dictatorship became the more determined were the people to oppose it.

This was the first example of a repressive regime that the Israelites would have to face. More would come in future years in the lands of Israel, Spain, England, Russia and Germany, and on each occasion blame would be levied on the Israelites for no honest reason followed by repressive action. Marks made in stone within caves in Egypt where some Israelites frequented during their years of hardship implore aid from their one God, "El Shaddai", to lift from them the burden of slavery. That help would come unexpectedly, but not for some time.

At the foot of the 10th Pylon at Karnak, referred to as "The Great Edict of Horemheb" a stele was placed recording the king's decree to re-establish order in the two lands that made up Egypt, dividing power between Upper and Lower Egypt, between "The Viziers of Thebes and Memphis respectively" emphasising the importance the king placed on domestic reform.

The purpose of Horemheb's reforms was said to curb what he claimed were the abuses of power and privilege that a few individuals had achieved and the wealth they had amassed in their own hands, but his real object was to wrest any power away from the professionals and leaders of society and bring the whole country under his own control.

In every successful nation you will always find some measure of corruption, and ancient Egypt was no exception to the rule. It is unlikely the corruption was as great as Horemheb declared but he had to find some excuse to carry out his plan to remove the

Horemheb

Israelites from Egyptian society without having to face a backlash from the people, and exaggeration of the problem was the approach he took. There was no proof that the Israelites were involved in corruption but they were useful scape goats to take the blame. His 'Great Edict', which he had placed in a most prominent position for all to see, gave him the excuse to take action. Where Amenhotep III ordering the killing of the new-born boy children of the Israelites had failed to resolve was the problem, Horemheb was determined to succeed. He not only took away their freedom but confiscated their wealth, explaining that it was only just that they should pay for all the trouble they had caused.

The people reacted by paying lip service to the directives of the Pharaoh simply to avoid being reported by spying neighbours for not complying without demur. They objected to the enslavement of the Israelites who had not committed any crime and were innocent of the allegations made against them. They believed that, although they could do nothing about the situation then, time would bring change for the better as it had done in the past. For the immediate future they would "ride out" the storm and await normality which they were sure would return to the country in time. They were to be sadly mistaken.

In the meantime they would do what they could to alleviate the suffering they saw being meted out to those who were their friends with small gifts of the necessaries of life given with the aid of bribes to the governors and overseers. This reminder of the kind and gentle attitude of the Egyptian people would be the subject of reward when the Israelites eventually gained their freedom.

To secure the future it is likely that Horemheb persuaded the priests of the Temple of Amun to make a pronouncement that the name of Amun should be included after each prayer to instil into the minds of the people the name of the "only true God". Just as the modern pronunciation of the name Tutankhamun is Tutankhamen, so Amen is the modern pronunciation of Amun. Ask a theologist the meaning of that word, and he will tell you that it is not known for sure, but that its translation is something like "and so be it", and no-one has been able to provide an alternative origin for this word. It is interesting to note that today so many of the religions of the world make use of the word "Amen" as the ending to each prayer. Old traditions die hard.

Horemheb's agenda was to secure total control of the country leaving no-one capable of challenging his authority, and the priests of the Temple of Amun were to be no exception to the rule. In restoring them to control of the religion they would no longer be permitted to carry out any further establishment duties which he gave to chosen members of the army on whose total loyalty he felt he could rely. To give him his due, he planned it well, and he was completely successful. Not forgetting the future, and appreciating that he would not have any children, he appointed from the army as his Grand Vizier a young officer called Paramesse to be his successor whom we know as Ramesses.

The Egyptian attitude to sound and effective government equated with two columns representing that of the kingly power on the left and the priesthood or establishment on the right, and, when those columns were conjoined by their deity, it secured protection for the people and gave strength and stability to the realm. By concentrating all power into the hands of a single individual, control took the place of harmony and pleasure; fear the place of loyalty and dedication.

Gone was Ma'at and the social order that provided the pleasure of living in friendship and harmony destroying any hope of achieving perfection in this life. In its place came a strict and ordered society where all lived in trepidation, and where the few appointed themselves as Gods enslaving the rest of the population to do their will.

CHAPTER 15

The Rise of a Great Leader

During this time, Moses had remained in the palace. Born during the reign of Amenhotep 111 and brought up in the house of a princess and daughter of the king, he had only peripheral personal knowledge of the attack on the people of his natural family and tribe. He spent his time at lessons and at play in the palace grounds excluded from the general public, and grew up with the princes and princesses of his age and other members of the royal family and the families of nobles. It was to a large extent a protected life with knowledge instilled into the child with the intention that he should take a leading role in the government of the nation in due time.

Amenhotep's children would have become his personal friends and social visits to their respective homes would have been common practice. Part of their training would have been to master the social graces of the lifestyle of the palace. Royal children would also have been taught languages, mathematics, geography, history and religion, but there would have been available to them other esoteric subjects from the world's most knowledgeable experts from astronomy to zoology. Young women had their special subjects in addition, but men had to spend time in the army, as they would have been expected to take a leading role in any necessary control of the land against insurgents or disputes with neighbouring tribes.

Part of their duties would also have been to visit all parts of Egypt not only to see for themselves the layout of the land and the procedures adopted for its defence, but also to be seen by the people to be taking an active role in ensuring for their protection at all times. From this they would understand the dangers of areas such as the desert and how it might be possible to survive there in the event of an emergency. In this way it would have been open to Moses to gather knowledge which would not have been available to the ordinary man.

Moses had the advantage of not being the subject of inter-marriage with all the medical problems that were derived from such relationships. He would have had an active mind and able to absorb all the learning that was made available to him. He was undoubtedly considered as a fine leader of men, a good army officer who was also popular with those he led and the people he met.

Even though it was well known that he was born of Habiru parents, he acted as an excellent Egyptian with all the airs and graces of a member of the royal family and was highly respected both as an individual and as a leader of men. It was of course known and accepted that he would never be able to take on the roles in the community reserved for royalty, but he was considered as a reliable and able officer and a gentleman of significant knowledge and ability.

Moses was interested in history, as is the wont of every good leader. It is likely that he had been introduced to leaders of the Habiru tribe from whom he had learnt stories of their exciting past that were attractive to every youngster, and they would have involved the history of the tribe and its formation all those generations ago. These stories were handed down from father to son, and in wanting a purpose to life he might well have spent his time recording these events. He had been

taught the art of writing in cuneiform script and would have
grown up knowing the Hebrew language because of his
natural family. Hebrew had the advantage of a form for each
letter rather than for each word, as in the Egyptian written
language, which made writing easier and for Moses such a
project would have been a pleasing pastime. Indeed he may
well have been concerned that no evidence of the contribution
that the Habiru had made to Egypt and the Egyptian people
was available, and he might well have felt that this absence of
such information needed to be rectified.

Thus, Moses set about writing down the history of the
Israelitish tribe. It is not surprising that the detail of the
earlier years is somewhat sketchy, because the stories that had
been passed from the older generations to the young were
often vague on detail of the earlier years and so much detail
was lost over time, but he did the best he could securing for
future generations all the information that was available
recording the important names of those who were to form the
basis of modern religious belief and in particular the salient
factor of a single unseen deity to whom all prayers were to be
directed.

He named this history the *Book of Genesis* which explains
how the Habiru tribe came to exist, the problems that they
had faced over the years and how they came to be in Egypt
and ends with the death of the man who had been so
successful for all the people of both nations, namely Joseph
whom the Egyptians knew as Zaphnath-Paaneah. He would
have had ample time for this achievement and very good
reason to concentrate on something that would keep him out
of trouble. The writing of this history would have taken a
considerable time and effort in research, but Moses had about
25 years to complete this project during the reigns of

Akhenaten, Neferneferuaten, Smenkhkara, Tutankhamun and Ai.

The political and social events that were taking place during that time were the cause of some upheaval, and Moses had watched the developments with some concern. The authorities were aware of his activities among the Habiru, but no action would have been taken in relation to his birth parents out of respect for his adoptive mother, the Princess Bithiah, who had no doubt warned him not to interfere with the will of the establishment and to concentrate his mind on other things. Indeed he was until then on the face of it no trouble. However, the repressive acts of Pharaoh Horemheb affected everyone, and life must have been one long worry in case Horemheb's spies overheard any hint of rebellion. Fear of reprisals made everyone a spy, and no-one could be trusted to keep any secret or not to report any possibility of treason. A failure to do so would have rendered a neighbour liable to conviction and reprisals on the whole family.

However, Moses was interested in his background and had become well known amongst the enslaved community. They liked him and looked upon him as the one person who could assist in times of the severest difficulty, their only contact with those who directed their lives. Clearly Moses had a genuine concern for the people who were his ancestors and may well have made some effort to reduce the severity of their servitude but without much success. His expressed sympathy with those upon whom the establishment considered were an adverse influence to the Egyptian people did not ingratiate him with the King who, given the excuse, would not have hesitated to make an example of such treachery.

Moses was aware that the suffering of the Habiru people was increasing and was frustrated by the fact that he was unable to take any action which might have alleviated their pain. King Horemheb was a tyrant who knew only repression as the way to control the people, and, if that did not work, he would simply increase the burden on the offenders. He was unable to understand that such a policy attracts only a determination for change and does not have any lasting effect on society.

In endeavouring to bring hope to the beleaguered Habiru Tribe their leaders had changed their name to Israelites, and far from accepting the traditional Egyptian Gods had strengthened their loyalty to their one God, El Shaddai. As was inevitable the King used this as an excuse to make the Israelites scapegoats for every wrong that the repressive regime faced and added ever-increasing burdens onto their shoulders. The Israelites had truly become slaves, and from their sad lives they could see no hope for the future. Horemheb had achieved his goal and this would remain the situation until his death after some 27 years. In a cave used by the slaves there remains a short prayer in Hebrew carved into a stone wall "Help me – El", a sign of utter despair.

Fired with hate for this contemptible Pharaoh who had destroyed a happy community, loyal to the crown with a peaceful way of living, he vented his anger on a member of the army. Like all male members of the palace Moses had been trained in the army and was a strong and fit man. He would have been well able to dispose of one soldier. When Moses found an Egyptian guard whipping one of the slaves, he lost his temper and killed the guard. He had thought that no-one had seen him save for the man he had saved, so he hid the body in the sand and left (Exodus Ch. 3 v.12).

It was therefore a great surprise to him when he returned the following day to hear from two of the Israelites who acted and spoke as if they knew about the killing. There are always those who vie to gain favour for themselves with their masters, and the two who approached Moses sarcastically asked why he was trying to be a prince over them suggesting that he might kill them as well (Exodus Ch.2. v.13). There was genuine fear that, when the authorities found the body of the murdered Egyptian, someone would be made to take the blame, so that they had no choice but to make the report in case this would give the Pharaoh the excuse of taking it out on the Israelites. The fact remains that they delayed reporting the matter and must have advised Moses to get out giving him time to escape before making their report. Moses realised that Horemheb was looking for an excuse to order his death, and at the age of 40 he had no choice other than to leave Egypt quickly and before the Pharaoh had time to order his arrest. In this way blame for the murder would fall on Moses and not the Israelites.

Moses had been taught methods of survival in the desert. It was the only way to go that would give him any chance of escape from the hands of this vicious King and the best place in which to disappear. Furthermore, he knew that, if he could reach the other side of the desert, there were tribes there who were not enamoured of the Egyptians. He had a horse and could lay his hands on some provisions which gave him some advantage. He also knew that it would be most unlikely that the King would have required any of his men to risk their lives by venturing into the danger that awaited anyone who took that path.

The Pharaoh was probably content to let him go, as it saved him the trouble and embarrassment of having to deal with Moses which he knew would have been unpopular. As a token gesture Horemheb put out a directive that a criminal member of the Royal Court was being sought for the crime of murder, and anyone found harbouring him would suffer severe punishment if they were caught. But Horemheb was probably pleased with this incident, as Moses had played into his hands and another area of opposition to his scheme had been annihilated without him having to take any overt action to achieve that end. All appeared to be going his way, and he quickly forgot about this so-called prince who was such an anomaly in the Court.

Thus it was that Moses through sheer strength of body and character arrived in Midian where he came across a number of young girls trying to water their sheep at a well and in need of protection from neighbouring shepherds. He came to their aid, and with his army training they were no match for him. The girls' father, Jethro, who had heard from passing traders that a prince had left Egypt in disgrace realised who he was and being indifferent to the Egyptians and to the price on his head, expressed his gratitude to Moses and offered him a place of rest. Moses found peace of mind in this quiet corner of the world with a kindly and loving family, and he married one of Jethro's daughters, Zipporah, and remained there in hiding until the right time arose for him to return to Egypt.

CHAPTER 16

A New Military Regime

In about the year 1292 BC after a reign of some 27 years, Horemheb died, and the news of his passing spread quickly throughout the Middle East. Quite early on in his reign Horemheb had realised that he was not going to have children. There could have been any number of reasons for this. As an army man through and through he had spent his whole life with men and very possibly did not like women or there could have been medical reasons for his failure to father a child. This realisation may well have exacerbated his attitude towards the people, as his demeanour became ever more single-minded as the years went by.

It is likely that he suffered from a delusional psychosis that a nation can only be made great by a total control of its people. He had no understanding of what makes a great leader and no concern for or interest in history that might have guided him to the experience of those who had achieved so much for Egypt in the past. He knew the ancestors by name and their successes by reputation but was not interested in how they achieved so much in so short a time.

One way or another Egypt had experienced a dictatorship of extreme proportions, and for the people the antithesis of every aspect of the Code of Conduct. Any protest was put down with vigour, and his ill-temper was taken out on those who had been enslaved, ever increasing the burdens he had placed on their already meagre lives. The Israelites had become the ultimate scapegoats with no way out. Under Horemheb's command the army treated them with utter contempt, and any attempt at escape would be punished with such severity on so many that prayer was all that was left to them.

In fact there could be no practical way to escape without help from outside, and in the eyes of those who daily faced the object of the King's unrelenting hostility that would take a miracle. They were not permitted any contact outside their restricted area in which they were guarded day and night. Anyone offering any assistance to the slaves would, if caught, suffer the same punishments as those who tried to escape as a warning to others not to get involved. In any event there was nowhere to go or hide, and in the unlikely event that they were able to reach the desert only death from starvation and dehydration awaited them. The Israelites were for all practical purposes doomed to be worked to death on menial projects.

But some remembered Moses who had sworn that he would return and bring them to safety. It was little enough to go on, but it gave just a glimmer of hope. Moses would have to have survived the desert and been taken in by friendly tribesmen. If he had survived all those years, he would also no longer be a young man, and, whilst all those years ago he was a great general and leader of men, Moses did not have an army to match that of the Egyptians. But there were still some who clung to that scrap of hope which kept them going.

Horemheb was absolutely satisfied that he had brought order, justice and equality to the lives of the Egyptian people and had removed from their midst a cancer in the form of the Israelites for which in time they would be eternally grateful. Even if they did not realise it then, there would come a time when they would appreciate the vast improvement over the life of injustice and corruption that had been prevalent for years under those monarchs before him whom he had served from Akhenaten to Tutankhamun who in his eyes were weak and insipid rulers.

With this in mind he contrived to ensure that he would provide a new and enlightened dynasty of tough, determined men with a military background who would have no time for people who did not conform to the strict rules he would impose. Thus, he chose from the army someone who mirrored his own rise to power whom he could trust to carry on the good work that he had begun. He selected a man called Paramessu who was the son of a battalion commander, starting his career as an ordinary soldier, winning his commission on his own ability and rising to the rank of general. He had distinguished himself as an assistant to senior officers giving them unflinching support and about whom they had given excellent reports and later distinguishing himself as a fortress commander.

Horemheb had found just the man he was looking for to be his successor. This was an individual who had distinguished himself under great pressure in the army and who could be trusted to continue the detailed control over the nation that was clearly needed if Egypt was to survive. There were too many tribes on the borders of the land who were growing in strength and only waiting for the opportunity of attacking. In his opinion the showing of the slightest weakness would trigger an attack from all sides, and this could only be countered by a show of massive strength.

Paramessu was for him the obvious choice of succession, but he would need training, and Horemheb arranged to bring him into the palace as his aide. For this Paramessu had to give up all his then titles but was eventually promoted to "King's

Deputy and Vizier" and eventually to "King's Son", thereby
ensuring his hereditary right to the throne.

Thus, although Horemheb was the founder of this new
approach to kingly authority, he was promoting a new dynasty
for which there would be the new name of "Ramesses", and
Paramessu was to become Ramesses 1. Horemheb was
encouraged in his choice as his protégé who was not a young
man by the time he came to the throne, as he already had sons
and grandsons who would secure the monarchy under rulers
who were, to his mind, bound to take the nation to new great
heights. Pharaoh Horemheb died having achieved all he had
set out to do, and for the next 230 years over the 19th and 20th
Dynasties, although there were kings with other names, it was
the name of Ramesses that would dominate the monarchy
until the death of Ramesses X1.

CHAPTER 17

The Rise of a Legend

Moses had throughout his sojourn in Midian which lasted for some 25 years led the life of a shepherd, but he hankered to return to Egypt to find out about his family. He had for some time been anxious about his natural parents, and the one woman to whom he owed his life, the Princess Bithiah. He also wanted to know how the Israelites had fared during their bondage.

At first he was reluctant to go in case the news of the King's death was inaccurate for fear that this was a ruse by Horemheb to get him to return and to face punishment, but the rumours continued to circulate that there was a new Pharaoh who had ascended the throne whom he did not know, and it was always possible that he might be persuaded by signs and warnings to release the Israelites to enable them to make a sacrifice to their God. Even though sceptical, Moses was attracted to the idea of a challenge and had the feeling that this could work.

Moses felt that in the turmoil that was always created with the advent of a new king he could quietly slip into Egypt, and dressed as a shepherd would not be recognised too easily. There were always traders from other countries who would enter the markets, and he would just be another one of them. It was also probable that any witness to the murder of the Egyptian taskmaster which was the reason why he had escaped was no longer available to give evidence, so that prosecution was unlikely particularly if it was indeed true that there really was a new Pharaoh who would only have known Moses by reputation.

The return of Moses to Egypt came as a shock to the whole community, both Egyptian and Israelite alike. His hope to keep this event quiet and just to enjoy the company of his natural and adoptive family and his close friends was dashed to the ground within a short space of time. The Israelites had been praying for a deliverer from their burdens, and the Egyptians from the consequences of a heartless dictator. There was no-one left in the royal family of the 18th Dynasty to take the throne and Horemheb had foisted on them an army officer who was a mere commoner without any of the learning and abilities afforded to the royal family. Many would have looked on Prince Moses who had grown up with those advantages as a possible king who would have been able to reintroduce Ma'at – the true mode of Egyptian life and to restore equilibrium to their beleaguered existence.

It was with this in mind that all the people gave an unexpected welcome to their popular Prince even though he had returned in the garb of a shepherd and was already a man of senior age being supported by a crook or staff rather than how they remembered him as a true Prince of the Land. It was well known that he had a stutter and found it difficult to communicate, but their experience with Horemheb and the advent of his successor so carefully trained by him in his vicious and uncompromising approach to kingship led them to believe that Moses had been sent by the Gods to release them from this oppressive regime.

Thus Moses supported by his brother Aaron came to be invited to an audience with the new Pharaoh, Ramesses 1, who had by then been on the throne for only a few months.

This new King who had heard of the Prince Moses and his exploits and would have been in some awe of a man who had stood up to Horemheb and had escaped his clutches, had to find a way of facing up to a man who could be King in his place. It took Moses only

Stone head carving of Ramesses I,

minutes to size up this excuse for a monarch who appeared to be a weak and insipid reflection of his predecessor. There was simply no comparison with Moses and his strength of character and leadership skills.

Ramesses was in a dilemma, because he could not ignore Moses, and, as he had not committed any crime for which he could be charged, the King had no reason to order his arrest. Indeed, the popularity which had been shown towards Moses might well have triggered a riot if any untoward action had been taken against him. The King decided to invite Moses to the Court and to turn him into a character of amusement to show the people that this was no alternative King in the making and certainly not one who could provide the Israelites with any hope.

Moses arrived with Aaron in support in answer to the invitation and the King pointed to his garb with a measure of contempt suggesting that he did not look much like a Prince of Egypt. Moses replied that he was not and never had been interested in being in line to the throne and that he only wanted to bring the Israelites out of Egypt to enable them to offer a sacrifice to their God. Obedience to their God was necessary to obviate punishment to those who failed to comply or who put a barrier in the way to enable them to do so.

The King replied that he did not recognise their God who could not be seen and wanted proof that he existed. Moses had learned some of the tricks played by the priests at party times and made use of them to worry the King which did result in some panic but this was not going to cause the King to change his mind. To show that he would not lose face before the people, the King followed the teaching of Horemheb and ordered that the burden on the Israelites should be increased by making them collect the straw that went into making the mud bricks they used in road and building construction without reducing their daily quota. The message to the slaves was an attempt to show that all Moses could do was to fail in his endeavour to get them released and to add to their burden. This might well reduce his popularity and get him chased out of Egypt.

This small setback did not deter Moses even though many questions were raised as to his abilities. As he had been taught in his youthful years he had planned for what he had assumed would occur, and there is little doubt that he already knew of the advance of poisonous red vegetation which was occasionally released into the upper part of the Nile close to its source causing serious problems to the food chain. Indeed Moses had visited Nubia and knew the Kushite community well, and he was aware that they were no friends to the Egyptian command and that it would not have taken much persuasion for them to have lent their assistance by ensuring that the maximum amount of the poisonous vegetation was sent on its way down river.

It is likely that he had made such an arrangement with them before entering Egypt ascertaining how long it would take for the poisonous bright red vegetation which happened naturally from time to time to arrive at Thebes, so that it appeared at the right time in Egypt with all the consequences about which he had learned as a young man from the experts at the palace. Only those who had taken a special interest in such subjects would have been open to such knowledge, and the King and his courtiers would not have been among them.

It is possible that the priests of the Temple of Amun would have known about this advent, but they were no longer in the employ of the King as civil servants and efforts had been made to cut off any extra income they used to receive in earlier years from wealthy Egyptians. They had also learned to be wary of speaking about any possible disaster which might befall the nation for fear that the King would find a way to put the blame on them. They stayed quiet and waited with interest to see what Prince Moses would do to belittle this new upstart of a ruler.

To prepare for his planned attack on this Egyption king, Moses sent on his family to Egypt, where they would be looked after by his family there. He travelled to Nubia to arrange his first onslaught to be put into effect.

Vegetation, known as Burgundy, Blood Algae or Oscillation Rubesceus, grew at the source of the Nile, then in Nubia, and still grows there today. It is known that from time to time lumps of this plant break away and float down the river. Going past Thebes, the river's pace slows and, in dying, the plants multiply massively and exude a bright red substance as they die and poisons river life and sinks to the bottom. As with all vegetation it creates carbon dioxide which is retained by the weight of the plants

The Cushites hated the Egyptians and were excited by the thought of causing some degree of pain on them. To ensure that the vegetation arrived at the right time, he took a Nubian princess with him to Egypt who would return to signal when to release the vegetation.

To ensure that no-one had any warning of this plan, Moses said that he had married the princess to give a reason for her to accompany him, which caused a serious argument with his sister, Miriam, who berated him for taking a second wife. Miriam accused him of acting like an Egyptian prince and failing to to comply with Hebrew law of having only one wife. Moses was pleased with the reaction because it took minds away from his real plan and gave him the excuse for sending the princess back to Nubia at the appropriate time.

The Nubians did not need any further encouragement to act and, on the return of their princess, set about cutting the vegetation and sending it on its way. Indeed, in their enthusiasm, they sent a vast quantity down the river, which coloured the water from one bank to the other, turning the river bright red and storing an immense quantity of carbon dioxide beneath the surface.

Moses and Aaron returned to Ramesses to warn him of impending disaster which would be meted out on the people if he continued to disobey God, but this new King, as Moses had guessed, was endeavouring to prove himself to the people and the neighbouring tribes who would be looking for signs of weakness in the establishment of a new monarch for the nation. He was not going to give in to a bunch of slaves led by a shepherd, and he laughed at the threat. Moses had timed his confrontation with Ramesses well for he did not have to wait long for the red poison in the river to appear. That would have a serious effect not only on the drinking water but also temporarily poisoning the food. All there would suffer from these consequences; and worse, the King would be embarrassed.

On the advice of Moses, the Israelites had prepared for the deadly vegetation by preserving enough water for their needs and food for their tables, but even they could not avoid the problems that followed. Fish died in the water and because of the poison could not be eaten, frogs left the water in droves seeking refuge in the houses and the fields, flies were attracted to the rotting corpses, and the people and cattle suffered from biting insects, lice and boils.

On each occasion Ramesses, who was simply not attuned to dealing with problems of this nature, became more irritated and more intransigent. He had persuaded himself that Moses was not going to win this contest and would soon run out of tricks and life would return to normal once again. Horemheb would not have stood for this kind of nonsense and nor would he. The advent of heavy hail with fire is not an unknown phenomenon where volcanic eruptions of a certain kind take place, and volcanic activity was common at that time in the Middle East. Perhaps Moses did have some knowledge provided to him by others to enable him to make such a threat, but the timing was crucial to keep the pressure on this intransigent king.

Equally so, with the arrival of locusts whose flight towards Egypt may well have been prompted by the volcanic and seismic activities taking place. Both had the effect of destroying crops and structures upon which the Egyptian people relied for their wellbeing. Darkness from a volcanic cloud for a number of days would have frightened the people who were used to seeing blue skies, and this would have triggered thoughts of omens from the Gods for which the King was responsible in the eyes of the people.

At each event Ramesses showed ambivalence in first agreeing to let the Israelites go, and then, when the problem subsided, changing his mind. To him this was a game which he was beginning to enjoy and which he was quite satisfied he would win, because Moses was bound to run out of ideas when the natural progression of daily life would return, and peace restored to the land. But Ramesses had not appreciated that all this was leading to one more plague that would dramatically change the picture and devastate both him and the whole nation. All the others had caused some discomfort, but had not had any permanent effect giving the opportunity for the Pharaoh to enjoy his games.

For the King the threats that Moses had made had little, if any, effect on his daily life because he had ample staff to look after his needs and those of the palace hierarchy. But each plague visited on the people left the Egyptians feeling that they could no longer befriend the Israelites and sympathy for them had waned. The King decided to play a trump card to bring the game to an end in his favour. His advisors related to him the resounding effect Amenhotep 111 had on the Israelites when he ordered the death of all the first-born Israelitish male children and how that gave him the opportunity of bringing those people under control.

He repeated that edict and by this one act considered that he had aligned himself with the great monarchs of the past. What he did not realise was that this was part of the plan that Moses had for him and the Egyptian people, and he told the King that he had just pronounced his own punishment for disobedience of the will of God. This final punishment would devastate families throughout the city and leave a permanent scar on the whole of the nation. Moses knew this and told the Israelites to prepare for leaving Egypt with urgency.

CHAPTER 18

Exodus at Last

The rotting vegetation had sunk to the bottom of the river where the water was left in still pools and that created carbon dioxide which was held amongst the vegetation at the base of pools in the river. It was the custom of the first born of each family to sleep in the open on the roof of the houses, as that was the coolest place. The first born of the King also took that advantage. It would take very little to disturb the vegetation in the water, and carbon dioxide being lighter than water but heavier than air would quickly rise to the surface of the river and be taken by the light evening breeze across the city travelling low over the houses suffocating those who slept on the roofs. This unusual phenomenon occurred in recent times in the Cameroon with devastating effect to both the people and animals.

Thus the King and the people of Egypt woke to find their first-born dead, and the King was now to face the wrath of the people on whom they had relied for their protection. He had failed them. He had played the game and lost, and everyone around him knew it. He had been belittled by a mere shepherd and a bunch of slaves and each of the families had been punished as a result of his stupidity and incompetence. They demanded that he get rid of the slaves as quickly as possible, and he ordered Moses to leave Egypt immediately with all the Israelites.

He was tempted to rain devastation on the slaves to teach them that disobedience to the King was not an option for them, but he was so confused by the events that had taken place, he just wanted to rid himself of this troublesome shepherd and insolent servants. He was advised that attempting to murder the Israelites whilst they were in Egypt might have brought a further disaster on him and the people, so that was not an option. In any event he wanted time without this ex-prince to mourn for the loss of his own son.

Moses had already planned for the evacuation of all the people with their belongings. Before leaving Midian, he had the basis of a plan prepared. During his time in Midian, he had met up with those of the Habiru tribe who had remained in the Land of Canaan to be prepared to meet those who would be leaving Egypt under his command. They were a good fighting force and would provide the protection that would be needed at the border on their escape.

In his army training Moses had learned that planning was crucial to the movement of a considerable number of people. It was difficult enough to plan with a fighting force of disciplined and well-trained men, but this was a very different project and would have taken an exceptional individual to have organised such an evacuation. There were some 600,000 people to move with all their belongings and animals some of whom were old and some very young and all had to be catered for and protected. Speed and organisation were of the essence. Moses realised that he had to reach the border with Canaan before the King changed his mind where he would meet with the Habiru fighters.

Of course he could not have achieved this alone, and he had searched for and found a number of leaders among the Israelitish tribe on whom he could place the burden of responsibility for the detailed arrangements that had to be made. By this time the people had total trust in him and were willing to obey his every wish. He told each household the night before the last plague had struck to kill and cook a lamb so that they had a good meal before leaving the following morning with food for the journey and to pack their households ready to leave at very short notice.

They would also spread the blood of the lamb on the doorposts of their dwellings so that those who were joining them on their trek north would be easily recognisable to those who were placed in charge of each street thus ensuring that none who were to join them were left behind. He also appointed the leaders of the twelve tribes of Israel to ensure that everyone was offered whatever help and transport that might be needed so that the elderly and infirm would not be overlooked. This alone was a task of major significance which under the command of one of the greatest leaders the world has ever known would be achieved with comparative ease to the consternation and amazement of those in Egypt who witnessed the operation.

Moses and Aaron had been summoned to the palace to be brought before the King who had understood that it was his own decree that had caused the devastating effect of the killing of the first-born of the Egyptian people. He had been faced with blame from the people of Egypt who had demanded that he rid them of these hateful Israelites. Ramesses realised that he had been fooled into making the wrong decisions and was no doubt endeavouring to find a way of blaming others for the hurt that had been caused to his nation. He had wanted to make Moses a laughing stock among all the people, and instead it was now he who had to face the music. He demanded that Moses and his Israelites leave the land immediately intimating that anyone who remained would suffer.

That was why it was so important for a well-planned escape to be put into effect without any delay. Still there would have been some amongst the Israelites who for one reason or another would refuse to go with them, but equally there were many Egyptians realising the reactions of this wild and uncontrolled King might have who would join the ranks of those leaving, not the least of whom was the Princess Bhitia and her entourage whose kindness and generosity was of assistance to so many on the journey.

It would take a few days to bring the large numbers of escapees to the meeting point with the Habiru warriors at the crossing of the "Yom Suf" (literally "the Sea of Reeds" but incorrectly translated as the "Red Sea"). There were about 600,000 of them at the time and most were on foot. The King and his nobles would have wanted time to grieve for the loss of their eldest sons, but Moses knew that this would only give him just enough time to conclude the escape from Egypt. The King had at his disposal 600 chariots which formed the basis of his army, and he would not hesitate to use them once he had collected his thoughts and began to think of revenge.

The event of the plagues and the method of escape to the north being the shortest and easiest route across the Yom Suf can be explained by volcanic and seismic activity in the area which could very easily have produced the effects intimated in the Book of Exodus. This route taken may also have been a ruse intended to lead the Egyptians to believe that they were travelling directly into Canaan before they turned east towards Midian along the caravan route.

The crossing was comparatively close to Goshen where the slaves had been housed. There is a village there today known as "Tuf", and that is the pronunciation of the word for reeds in both Egyptian and Hebrew. Today the actual place of the crossing is covered by a concrete roadway because the surface of the land has risen. In those days the land was lower and the water covered the whole area. For the people to have crossed amongst the reeds with their carts and animals would have been a mammoth task, so that the movement of the pool of magma lifting the ground would have enabled the multitude to have crossed on dry land.

Once the magma had been exhausted from that pool, the ground began to sink and the sea would have rushed in. Anyone crossing at that time would have been caught with devastating effect if they had been clothed with full armour. The Egyptian army in their chariots would not have stood a chance. With the King at the head of his army there is every reason to believe that he would have suffered the fate of drowning as the final blow against him. Some of his army would have been able to escape only to return to Thebes with the tale that those whom the King had oppressed stood and watched him die and the powerful Egyptian army belittled by a bunch of slaves.

That is the story from the Bible. It is not surprising that Egyptian history does not record anything of that nature. It was only permissible to have recorded great acts and deeds of the monarch of the time, and this was a failure of immense proportions for this unpopular King. The fact remains that he lasted for only 17 months on the throne of Egypt, and there is no record of how he died. When his time came, he was not a young man, and we know that he already had several grandchildren when he became the Crown Prince during the final years of Pharaoh Horemheb, but he was only in his late 30s and should have had a significant life ahead of him. To have ridden on a chariot chasing the escaping slaves would not have been a possibility for a man very much older, but it is not surprising that at that age he would have found it immensely difficulty to escape from the trap into which he hurled himself with his chariots out of uncontrolled rage.

Ramesses 1 whose mummified body is now in the Cairo Museum was the Pharaoh of the Exodus, and perhaps one day it will be possible to gain some proof of this by DNA testing. The date was 1290 BC, just 17 months after his accession to the throne, and the Children of Israel would from then wander in the desert for roughly 40 years during which time they would shed those who had the mindset of slaves and build an army with the capability of meeting the challenges that awaited them in the "Land of Milk and Honey" which had been promised to them.

Moses was keen for the Israelites to build a new homeland in the Land of Canaan, but he realised that this could not succeed without a cohesive and well-trained band of fighters led by officers who were respected. To bind this group of dissident and argumentative rebels into a team of single-minded and enthusiastic achievers he forged a new approach based on the well tried and tested "Ma'at", the Code of Conduct, which had served the Egyptian people so successfully over some 3,000 years, and to ensure that they had a distinctive individuality he provided special procedures in a new religion with a distinctive festival to recall and commemorate the great events that they had experienced in Egypt, but with specific requirements that were intended to distinguish them from all other nations.

As the new generation grew up, the social and religious procedures brought a cohesion to the people turning them into an extended family who could be led into the new phase he had planned which would make them a nation. Until then the people had kept to the desert to the east of Canaan fearful of those who occupied the land there. Now Moses was ready to plan the campaign that would rid the land of the tribes that would oppose him and to build a mighty nation. Those who would befriend them would be welcomed within the boundaries of the Land of Israel, but some would fight, and they would have to be annihilated.

Sadly, by this time Moses had reached the end of his life. He knew that he had imparted to the new leaders of the people and the officers of his army the wealth of knowledge that he had learned in Egypt that would stand them in good stead. There was no doubt in his mind that they would succeed in their endeavours, and his last moments witnessed their crossing into the Land of Canaan.

Moses had achieved something which very few, if any, could ever have done. He took a group of downtrodden and beaten slaves and forged them into a nation which would last for longer than any of the great nations the world has experienced. He was born a Hebrew and brought up as an Egyptian Prince; a natural leader he brought the best to his people and gave them the future for which they had prayed. That future was formulated from that extraordinary mix of Hebrews and Egyptians which had brought such perfection to the lives of all the people in the 18th Dynasty and which some still endeavour to emulate today through religion and freemasonry.

CHAPTER 19

Verification of the Facts

In Genesis Ch. 15 v.13 Abraham is told that the Children of Israel would continue to be strangers in a "foreign land" that is not theirs for a period of 400 years during which time they would become servants to the host nation but that thereafter they would return in the fourth generation. This was an estimate calculated from the date Abraham entered Canaan. In Exodus Ch. 12 v. 40 the actual period of time was stated to have been 430 years. This was from the time Abraham had first arrived in Canaan to the time Joseph and King Ahmose extended the invitation for the family and entourage to reside permanently in the Land of Goshen in Egypt, some three and a half generations, 200 years would have passed. Between Joseph and Moses there were four generations which would have accounted for the remaining 230 years.

The best information we have is that Joseph was sold into slavery when he was 17 which would have been in the year 1542 BC, and that he was appointed Grand Vizier over all Egypt when he was about 30 years of age.

After seven years a famine arose in the Middle East just as he had predicted, and it must have been about two years later that the Habiru (or some of them) came to settle in Goshen which would have been in the year 1520 BC. On the basis of a sojourn in Egypt for 230 years, the exodus must have taken place in 1290 BC.

Ramesses I had ascended the throne in 1292 BC and died 17 months later in 1290 BC in circumstances that are unknown and unexplained particularly bearing in mind that, although a grandfather, he was not old and he was clearly a fit man

There have been many attempts made to calculate the date when the Children of Israel left Egypt, some placing the date as far back as 1440 BC in an endeavour to suggest that the Hyksos were really the Habiru by another name. However, that would not take account of the fact that the Habiru were put to work on the construction of the two store cities of Pithom and Pi-Ramese which were not started until the reign of Amenhotep 111.

Others suggest that God would not have taken on any Pharaoh; it would have had to be the most powerful and thus they conclude that it could have been none other than Pharaoh Ramesses II. Again this could not have been so, because Ramesses I1 did not ascend to the throne until 1279 BC, and he did not die until some 66 years later, in 1213 BC which would have meant that King Solomon could not have been King in Israel until 733 BC, and this does not accord with the best information we have which is that Solomon could not have acceded to the throne after 800 BC.

Another proposal is the Akhenaten was the Pharaoh of the Exodus on the basis that he was considered the heretic king and would have been releasing the people who supported his own belief. This argument fails as we know that Akhenaten did not die from drowning and work was still to be done on the two store cities.

All these ideas have some interesting and forceful arguments in some respects, but these suggestions do require us to ignore the known facts and overlook the personalities of those involved and the reasons for the decisions they made. Also they do not accord with the guiding dates and facts given in the Bible.

So often those who endeavour to lend support for a new and interesting scenario find themselves having to change the known facts and alter existing evidence or dates. No-one can be absolutely accurate as to dates during this period of history, and total reliance cannot be placed on the exact number of years mentioned. The estimates and facts given may or may not be accurate, but equally cannot be ignored or assessed in some way to suit any given theory. They have to be given some credence which does lead to certain conclusions that assist in determining the date of the Exodus and the Pharaoh involved, and it is not unreasonable to assume that the changes taking place in Egypt at the time had a direct effect on the events described in the Bible, and the dates do lend verification to the Exodus having taken place in 1290 BC.

This view is also supported by another event referred to in the Bible. The Habiru slaves were involved in the building of the two store cities of Pithom and Pi-Ramese started during the later years of the reign of Amenhotep III and were still not finally completed in the reign of Horemheb which alone would count against any suggestion that the Exodus took place before Horemheb died. Store cities would not require the same level of expertise as other projects, and it would have been acceptable for most of the work to be carried out by lower grade workers.

Approaching the calculation from the other way, Kings 1 Ch. 6 records that 480 years passed between the Exodus and the fourth year of the reign of King Solomon when the building of the Temple was started. There has been some question as to this estimate of time, but it is unlikely that would be completely misconceived.

If the Exodus took place in the year 1290 BC, by adding 480 years, it would place Solomon on the throne of Israel in the latter part of the 9th Century BC, with Solomon being born in the year 826 BC and acceding to the throne in 814 BC at the age of 12. It would follow that the building of the Temple would have commenced four years into his reign in 810 BC and would have been completed seven years later in 803 BC.

The current best estimate for the reign of King Solomon was in the earlier part of the 10th Century BC with the Temple being built in about 960 BC. Taking account of the 480 years mentioned in the Book of Kings the Exodus would have taken place in 1440 BC during the reign of an earlier Pharaoh. This would not have accorded with the building of the cities of Pithom and Pi-Ramese nor with the other events that were taking place at the time.

It is possible, as some have suggested, that the estimate of 230 years that the Hebrews sojourned in Egypt was exaggerated particularly as it was intimated that this was intended to span only four generations. However, that estimate is more likely to be accurate as it is distinctly possible that Moses himself wrote or had a hand in writing the Books of Genesis whilst he was in Egypt and the Book of Exodus during the 40 years in the desert, whereas the remaining three books of the Pentateuch were probably not written until the sojourn of the Israelites in Babylon several hundred years later.

Some experts maintain that in those days a generation was considered as being about 40 years, and some maintain that a generation at the time was only 30 years on the basis that they did not live that long due to quarrels, fighting and ill health. It is possible that this was then so in Egypt, but this would be surprising when one realises that the Bible mentions that Abraham lived to the grand old age of 175, Isaac to 180, and Joseph to 110. Perhaps the length of life was already reducing by the time the Habiru went to live in Egypt, but the estimate of roughly 55 for a generation appears to be perfectly viable, as is the estimate of 480 between the Exodus and the commencement of work to build King Solomon's Temple which spanned 12 generations in Israel.

The Bible also tells us that God aimed to induce a reluctant Moses to return to Egypt by mentioning that all the witnesses to the incident of the murder of the Egyptian guard and the Pharaoh from whom he had escaped had died, and that the new Pharaoh knew Moses only by reputation.

This could easily have been Ramesses I who may have heard of the Prince Moses and his exploits and would have been in some awe of a man who had trained as a Prince in Egypt and stood up to Horemheb. At the time Moses re-appeared in Egypt Ramesses had only been on the throne for a few months and might well have been unsettled by the appearance of this unusual and popular figure.

The event of the plagues and the method of escape to the north being the shortest and easiest route across the Yom Suf ("Sea of Reeds" and not the "Red Sea") can be explained by volcanic and seismic activity in the area which might well have produced the effects intimated in the Book of Exodus. This may also have been intended to lead the Egyptians to believe that they were travelling into Canaan before they turned east towards Midian.

Ramesses I was followed by his son, Seti I, who undertook several military operations in Canaan and Syria which were intended to stamp Egypt's control on the area. That campaign would not have started until about 1285 BC, and the fact that the Hebrews were in the desert at the time avoided them having to come into contact with the then stronger and better-trained forces of the Egyptians.

After the death of Seti I, Ramesses II, became the Pharaoh in about 1279 BC, and in the early part of his reign he also took a force into Canaan to attack the Hittites whom he met at Kadesh. Although he claimed the battle to be an outstanding success, he made a number of serious tactical errors and was fortunate to come out alive. In fact he was only saved from the chaos he had created by poor leadership by the fortunate and unexpected appearance during the course of the battle of some of his troops whom he had dispersed elsewhere.

At best the result was a draw and actually ended in the first known written treaty between two nations. Despite his bravado Ramesses II was greatly weakened by this experience and never ventured into that area again with aggression.

The Children of Israel are said to have wandered in the desert for 40 years during which time they built an army enabling them to conquer Canaan. If this took them 10 years, it would have enabled them to start building their cities in about 1240 BC. After some 20 years by about 1220 BC they must have been reasonably well established and in control over part of the land securing their cities as best they could. The successor to Ramesses II, Pharaoh Merneptah, who ruled Egypt between 1213 and 1204 BC, wanted to remind the people of the then Land of Israel that it was still Egypt who ruled and took with him an army to enforce his will on those who resided there.

He ensured that there would be no opposition to his rule, and on his way back to Egypt made his mark by taking on the Israelites in battle securing victory. It is said that he took back with him as a token of his success the Ark of the Covenant the Israelites used to carry the Tablets of the Law of Moses which he had stored in one of his southern towns now in Ethiopia. For posterity, Merneptah recorded on a commemorative Stele his victories over a number of cities of Syro-Palestinian peoples which included Israel and for this reason this record is referred to as "The Israel Stele".

While Merneptah had on this occasion established control, the signs were already clear that forces of opposition were gathering strength and Egypt's days were numbered.

Israeli Stele

CHAPTER 20

The Bible as a Source of Knowledge

In so many respects the Bible is the only source of information about the events that took place during the years when formulation of modern religion was taking place. For so long Western civilisations have simply accepted the stories on the basis that the Book was written by the hand of God. However, in recent years it has become fashionable to question the reliability of its teachings on the basis that it produces nothing more than a series of unsupported and unlikely events.

Observations are made that the Old Testament in particular is really nothing more than a series of fables related simply to make a point and that it is therefore unlikely that any of the named individuals ever existed. As an example it is suggested that individuals could not have lived for the number of years quoted in the Bible. Modern scientists have concluded that the Bible in intimating that the Earth was formed in six days is a clear example of a lack of knowledge which could not have occurred if a deity had produced the written word.

It must be borne in mind that the stories had been passed down from father to son over so many years and it is most likely that it was Moses who first wrote down those stories in the Book of Genesis. He compiled the information from those in the Habiru Tribe and the information of the early years would necessarily have been confused and lacking in detail. Names and other information about the families who existed over the years prior to Abraham would undoubtedly have been sketchy, but they were not part of the story leading up to the Exodus which really started with the decision by Terah, Abraham's father, to leave their home in the City of Ur in the Chaldees and to travel a dangerous path in search of a new life in the Land of Canaan.

The events of that time were still fresh in the minds of the people and there is no reason to believe that Moses did not record them accurately. There would have been no point in endeavouring to embellish the events that took place, as the story was both interesting and exciting. Moses made the best of the introduction to those events in a style of writing that has attracted readers throughout the world over all the generations since.

It is also likely that the events that took place since the Habiru were living in Egypt were well known to him and confirmed from other sources within the palace in Egypt. Moses had little else to occupy his time in his younger years and may well have taken a pride in writing the Book of Genesis at that time.

It is equally likely that Moses would have written the Book of Exodus whilst in the desert. There the facts were recorded by him as they occurred, and there is every reason to think that he would have wanted to set down the facts without embellishment. Indeed looking at matters from a different angle it is not unreasonable to say that so far there is nothing set out in the Bible that has been proved to be wrong or inaccurate.

New facts are appearing almost on a daily basis which go to proving the events mentioned in the Bible. Recently the existence of King David who ruled in Israel has been confirmed by the finding of a number of seals used by him and his civil service for official documents. If the story of King David is true, the same must be said for King Solomon. The existence of both of these kings had been the subject of question previously.

Of course the Exodus itself has been questioned because so many efforts have been made to find some evidence of this momentous event and nothing has been discovered, leading many to express scepticism that the event ever occurred. The suggestion in the Bible is that some 600,000 slaves left Egypt but there is no record of such a momentous event in Egypt nor any artefacts found which might provide some verification of what happened.

First, it must be said that it would not have been considered an event worthy of recording by the Egyptian King as this would not have been considered a victory. Indeed quite to the contrary; the King had been made to look foolish by having to demean himself to the demands of a shepherd and a bunch of slaves, and it would not have been in his interests to have recorded such an event for posterity.

Secondly there has been some disparity as to where the crossing of the "Red Sea" took place. An extensive search has been made of the places which were considered obvious, and it is not surprising that they found nothing because the "Red Sea" was a mistranslation of the "Yom Suf" which is the Sea of Reeds. A rather more careful investigation of the area would have elicited a place by the same of "Tuf" which is very close to the Land of Goshen where the Israelites were housed. There have been significant changes in the environment there, but the possibility of finding any artefacts is not now viable, because the area where it is most likely that the crossing took place is now covered by a concrete roadway.

Sceptics say that this is a good reason for questioning the story which lies at the very heart of Western religions, which are clearly based on a fallacy. The fact remains that the Israelites were in Egypt, and, whilst there remains a dispute as to the dates, they did emerge to form the Land of Israel and to build a temple there, and this is confirmed by the Israel Stele which records the battle Egypt had with the Israelites under the leadership of Pharaoh Merneptah.

It is interesting that so many mistakes have been made by enthusiasts seeking to prove or disprove the stories in the Bible. Queen Cathryn of Russia, a seriously religious lady with ample funds to spend, built a monastery on a mountain in Saudi Arabia she thought was the Mountain of Moses where he spoke to God and received the Ten Commandments, and sadly the wrong mountain was chosen. That mountain lies in Egypt.

As with so many of these well-meaning enthusiasts they jump to conclusions on the flimsiest of evidence providing sceptics with ammunition for questioning the veracity of the events recorded in the Bible which is the only existing history of the Habiru tribe and which is of such importance to our Western civilisation.

With the efforts of archaeologists and historians our knowledge is advancing, and there is little doubt that all aspects of the Bible will eventually be proved to have taken place. This work is produced to show that with the present knowledge the events referred to in the Bible could have taken place and are commensurate with the Egyptian chronology of events that make up the 18th Dynasty which recorded how it rose from near annihilation to its most successful period, and this had been achieved in co-operation with a foreign tribe who had gladly offered their help in token of friendship shown to Abraham.

CHAPTER 21

Finding a Way to Preserve Ma'at

The ancient Egyptians of the 17th and earlier Dynasties had formulated a Code of Conduct they called Ma'at as the true way of life, part being spent in prayer to Almighty God, part in labour and refreshment, and part in serving another in time of need through which they had almost achieved their goal of the perfect life. Sadly, events changed their world, and the human failing of grasping for power took control of their lives leaving them bereft of the good and satisfying existence their predecessors had formulated and enjoyed. The army-trained monarchs of the Ramesses Dynasty introduced dictatorship and self-gratification destroying any hope of a return to a life seeking only good for the people.

Perhaps Akhenaten acted too quickly or simply lived before his time, but in any event acted unwisely, as the way in which he brought in his religious and social reforms triggered an extreme reaction by vicious men who did not have the learning or breeding to understand that a quest for absolute power must result in the failure of their society.

Horemheb might have thought that he had secured the future for the people of Egypt, but in fact his dictatorial and dogmatic approach spelt the beginning of the end. Ramesses II is often said to have been Egypt's greatest king remaining on the throne for 66 years and living until the age of 92, and causing the building of many massive structures and statues.

But in so doing he tore the heart out of the people and by the end of the 20th Dynasty ancient Egypt was never to rise again to the greatness it had previously achieved, not because of the size and height of its buildings or the great mass of wealth it had gathered, but rather through the lack of depth of thought in their approach to life by the dictatorial leaders of the 19th and 20th Dynasties.

People often wonder why great and powerful nations formed with the best intentions fade away after a period of time. It occurs when morality and ethics have lost their meaning and are replaced with corruption and dominance. We find this throughout history, and Egypt, Greece and Rome are but three obvious examples. What is worrying is that we also see it happening today within the European Union whose failure is occurring whilst we watch.

Egypt in its greatest age had formulated for the world Ma'at, a moral and ethical code of conduct that will in the course of time provide the opportunity of perfecting our existence in this life and is left to us as a preparation for whatever a future after-life lies in store for us. Pharaoh Horemheb and the Egyptian rulers of the 19th and later Dynasties discarded that approach to life in favour of a totalitarian state in which they appointed themselves as Gods subjecting their people to total dominance. As with all other similar regimes, it eventually failed, and a nation that had led the way for some 3,000 years decayed, was taken over and condemned to history.

Today we look on the past in Egypt with wonder and amazement at their great achievements, but their greatest success was how they managed to attract the people to accomplish what still appears to us today to have been impossible. The willingness of the whole community to be involved stemmed from the respect and admiration for their leaders and the love of their way of life. Confident in their identity, they accepted immigration into their society provided that the foreigners had the same ideals as they did and could accept their way of life.

The formula of Ma'at was carried out of Egypt by Moses with the Children of Israel, and it is significant that Western religions when adopting that Code have thrived. Occasionally leaders of religions have fallen into evil ways and in the name of God have committed serious and unforgiveable crimes against the people. But religion should not have to take the blame for the excesses of the few. Freemasonry has throughout the ages endeavoured to act as a beacon of light by keeping alive that Code for the benefit of the whole of the secular world. Against all the odds Ma'at still remains for us today should we choose to adopt it.

List of Egyptian Kings with Dates of Events

Period	Events in Egypt	Involvement of Others
Seventeenth Dynasty		
Numerous Kings		Emergence of Greece
Rahotep		
Nubkheperra Intef		Babylon sacked by the Hittites
Sobekemsaf II		
Seqenenre Tao I		
Seqenenre Tao II, 1545-1541	Skirmishes with the Hyksos. Murdered by Hyksos	Joseph sold as slave in Egypt, 1542
Kamose, 1541-1539	Killed in battle with Hyksos	
Eighteenth Dynasty		
Ahmose, 1539-1514	Famine weakens Hyksos. Hyksos defeated, wiped out	Joseph made Grand Vizier, 1529. Habiru occupy Goshen, 1520
Amenhotep I, 1514-1493	Valley of the Kings opened	
Thutmose I, 1493-1481	Conquest of Nubia	
Thutmose II, 1481-1479		
Hatshepsut, 1479-1458	Formation of Egyptian Navy. Massive building programme	Extension of trade including to Land of Punt
Thutmose III,1458-1426	Battle of Megiddo 1458 Egyptian empire extended north of Megiddo	End of Minoan civilisation
Amenhotep II,1426-1400	A step back to corruption	
Thutmose IV, 1400-1390	Egypt attains zenith of her fortunes	Israelites (Habiru) sharing in Egyptian successes become wealthy and increase in numbers

Amenhotep III, 1390-1353	Major building programme at Thebes Plans made for building of the two store cities of Pithom and Pi-Ramese	Killing of Israelite male children Moses born, 1370
Amenhotep IV/ Akhenaten, 1353-1336	Building of City of Armana Joint reign with Nefertiti	Enforced worship of the new unseen God, the Aten
Neferneferuaten and Smenkara, 1336-1332	Joint Monarchs Smenkara dies, 1333	
Tutankhamun, 1332-1322	Crowned King at the age of 9 Married Ankhesenamun	Had two still born children End of Royal Family
Ay, 1322-1319	Accedes to throne by marrying Ankhesenamun	
Horemheb, 1319-1292	Army takes power King could not father children	Enslavement of Israelites Moses kills Egyptian guard and escapes into desert
Nineteenth Dynasty		
Ramesses I, 1292-1290	Chosen from the army and trained by Horemheb	Moses returns to Egypt Exodus in 1290
Seti I, 1290-1279		
Ramesses II, 1279-1213	Battle of Kadesh, May 1274	Death of Moses, 1250 Israelite invasion of Canaan
Mereneptah 1213 - 1204	Invasion of Libia. Reference to battle with Israel 1209	Egypt faces stronger enemies and an uncertain future.

THE AUTHOR

Colin Jaque was born in London where he still lives with his wife and celebrated their golden wedding at the time this book was first published. They have two children and five grandchildren.

Colin is a solicitor specialising in commercial litigation, in particular Chancery work, which often involves investigating the history of events leading to the dispute. He was drawn to that speciality as it seeks to find solutions to apparently intractable problems.

He is not new to writing but his previous works relate to books he co-authored with a barrister which were then used as the official guide to chancery litigation.

His life-long academic interest in Ancient Egypt, its people, history and culture has led him to challenge widely held historical inaccuracies. Using his investigative experience; this book delves into the facts surrounding ancient Egypt on which he puts a new interpretation. He has also reconciled the Bible story in Genesis and Exodus into the known history of Egypt ensuring that nothing clashes with the known facts about the Hicksos, the Hittites, the Hivites and the Kushites. Freemasonry has also provided certain facets of history which have given an explanation to obvious gaps in public knowledge.

He recognises that he is unable to guarantee that the end result is absolutely accurate, but he believes that this fresher approach throws new light on previous understandings and provides reasons for the actions taken. Whilst appreciating why it was thought necessary to react in the questionable way that some of the monarchs did, he does not seek to excuse their behaviour other than to say that they did not have the learning and sophistication to know any better or to understand that they were laying the ground for destruction of the way of life they were seeking so hard to protect.

Printed in Great Britain
by Amazon